FUTURE REALITIES OF COALITION GOVERNMENTS IN SOUTH AFRICA

MZWANDILE MASINA

REFLECTIONS ON COALITION GOVERNMENTS IN THE METROS: 2016–2021

INTERVIEW with MZWANDILE MASINA

by MZILIKAZI WA AFRIKA

Future Realities of Coalition Governments in South Africa

ISBN: 978-0-620-93859-4 (print), 978-0-620-94403-8 (electronic)

Published by SAAPAM
Building 14, Room 154
Aubrey Matlala Road
Block L, Soshanguve
South Africa

E-mail: SAAPAM@tut.ac.za

ABOUT THE AUTHOR

Mzwandile Masina is the Executive Mayor of the City of Ekurhuleni and the ANC Ekurhuleni Regional Chairperson. He was formerly the Deputy Minister of the Department of Trade and Industry, where he had previously worked as the Director: Business Development and Customer Services. In 2012 he was appointed as the Chief Executive Officer of the Gauteng Film Commission. Prior to that, he was Chief Operations Officer at the Gauteng Department of Sport, Arts, Culture and Recreation. He has worked for Ntsika Enterprise Promotion Agency as Programme Manager responsible for Targeted Groups and Uthingo Management as General Manager: Empowerment.

Masina studied at the University of the Witwatersrand School for Public and Development Management as well as the University of Pretoria where he graduated with a Master's degree specialising in Entrepreneurship. He has attained numerous local short executive and development programmes where he gained knowledge and insight into various business management practices. He served as the General Secretary of the South African Youth Development Programme (SAYDEP) where he was responsible for policy input during the formation of the National Youth Commission.

Masina is a passionate political and social activist, committed to the pursuit of radical economic transformation as a panacea for the attainment of a national democratic society.

ACKNOWLEDGEMENTS

I wish to express sincere gratitude to the African National Congress for the opportunity to serve under a coalition government in the City of Ekurhuleni Metropolitan Municipality. Being entrusted with such a great responsibility has been extraordinarily humbling. I am thankful to the Regional Executive Committee leadership collective of Ekurhuleni Region, led by my brother and comrade, Thembinkosi "TK" Nciza who have held the fort under challenging circumstances but whose commitment to bettering the lives of South African people has never faltered.

The Mikki Xayiya Foundation was instrumental in the writing of this book. They believed in its vision from infancy and throughout its writing gave invaluable support without which the book could not have been completed.

The research team that worked on this book, led by Senior Researcher Malaika Mahlatsi, with Joseph Mudau and Arthur Shopola as Research Assistants, is deeply appreciated. I am also grateful to Ennia Nyamutsika-Mhlanga for providing administrative support and editing services to the team.

Professor Mashupye Maserumule played a vital role in helping to shape and strengthen the ideas in this book. His sharp but constructive criticism and willingness to engage with ideas, whether or not he agrees with them, distinguish him as the intellectual colossus that he is. The encouragement and support provided by Professor Busani Ngcaweni is also deeply appreciated.

I wish to thank Dr John Molepo and the South African Association of Public Administration and Management (SAAPAM) broadly, for the immeasurable support that they provided in ensuring that this book reaches an audience that needs to engage with its contents. More than this, I wish to thank the association for the critical role that it is playing in the ideational space.

I am thankful to the Political Management Team of the City of Ekurhuleni, which includes the Speaker of Council, Alderman Patricia Kumalo and the Chief Whip, Councillor Jongiziwe Dlabathi, for the immeasurable support they provided in the writing of this book.

Special mention must also be made of coalition partners in the City, as well as all participants in the metros and local municipalities across the country, who willingly sacrificed their time to participate in interviews and discussions that gave depth to the submission. Sello Pietersen is deeply appreciated for the extraordinary efforts that he made in sourcing relevant persons for interviews in the Free State Province.

Finally, I wish to thank my phenomenal wife, Sinazo Masina, and children for their inexhaustible faith in me. Their unconditional support is an anchor I could never do without.

INTRODUCTION

The 2016 local government elections in South Africa, held on 3 August 2016, marked a crucial turning point in the politics of the country. These fifth local government elections in democratic South Africa were characterised by a marked change in patterns of voting, and consequently, in the constitution of local government. A salient outcome of these elections, which informs this submission, was an unprecedented loss of power in the country's metropolitan municipalities by the governing African National Congress (ANC), which subsequently resulted in the formation of several coalition governments with opposition parties with simple majority. Prior to these elections, the ANC governed seven of the eight metros in the country, namely, City of Tshwane, City of Johannesburg, City of Ekurhuleni, Nelson Mandela Metropolitan Municipality, City of eThekwini, Mangaung Metro Municipality and Buffalo City Metropolitan Municipality. By the end of these elections, only the City of eThekwini, Mangaung Metro Municipality and Buffalo City Metropolitan Municipality were still being governed by the ANC. The remaining four were governed through coalitions, while the City of Cape Town remained firmly under the governance of the Democratic Alliance (DA), South Africa's biggest opposition party.

This seismic shift in power has had implications for local government at both a theoretical and practical level. And while many a coherent analysis has been made of the results and their causes, deeper reflection on their implication for the future of South Africa's political system, particularly by local government practitioners, has been scant. This raises serious concerns about how discourse on coming times is being framed (or not). We sit on the threshold of the sixth local government elections since the dawn of the new dispensation. On 27 October 2021, millions of South Africans will be casting their votes for a government of their choice, exercising their constitutionally enshrined right to self-determination. What lessons, if any, have been learned from the 2016 elections? And how, if at all, do they help us to prepare for the multiple scenarios that could potentially play themselves out?

Answering these questions is an important exercise in providing theoretical interventions for the various institutional and structural transformations that need to happen for South Africa's democracy to work effectively and to truly represent the will and aspirations of the people. But answering these questions is not a simple exercise, for they are not simple questions. It is an exercise that demands cogitation on the historic and contemporary constructs that inform the political milieu within which we operate. Situating the conversation within an historical context helps us to construct a barometer that traces the foundations of the evolution of the party-political system as we know it. In doing so, we can make concrete assertions about what needs to be done – and how.

The starting point of our reflections on coalition governments must perhaps be the Western Cape Province, where the political dynamic is historically layered in great complexity. Since the advent of democracy in 1994, the ANC has been the majority party in most municipalities across South Africa, apart from the Western Cape Province. The ANC was unseated by the DA in the 2009 local government election. The subsequent election in 2014 saw the party maintain its hold on power in the province with a significantly increased majority. The Western Cape Province, because of this complex political dynamic, has always been an important case study in power transference and now, more importantly, the subject of coalition governments. This is because at both the provincial and municipal level, its coalition governments have defined the political landscape far longer than has been the case in other parts of the country.

The construct of the Western Cape Province as a DA stronghold is a creation of recent history – but one that necessitates understanding if we are to make sense of how and why coalition governments are formed. Right up to 2004, the DA was an opposition party in the Western Cape Province, having received only 27 percent of the vote in the provincial ballot. The province was governed initially through a coalition of the ANC and the New National Party (NNP) – a coalition that was born following the 2004 election in which no party was able to achieve an outright majority. While the ANC had plurality of 45 percent of the votes, this was insufficient for the constitution of a provincial government, necessitating a coalition with the NNP, which had obtained 11 percent of the provincial vote. This coalition would be altered significantly the following year during the floor crossing period in which elected members of parliament, provincial legislatures and municipal councils could change their political parties while maintaining their elected seats. All members of the NNP crossed the floor and officially joined the ANC, giving the organisation an absolute majority and constitutional mandate to govern the Western Cape Province.

At the municipal level, the coalition dynamics also played themselves out in the 2006 local government elections, where, as with the provincial elections two years earlier, coalition governments had to be formed in order to constitute the municipal governments, including in the City of Cape Town Metropolitan Municipality. While the DA had plurality in the City, holding 90 of the 210 seats on the council, it did not have enough votes to constitute a government, thereby necessitating a coalition. Several smaller parties, including the African Christian Democratic Party (ACDP), the Freedom Front Plus (FFP), the United Democratic Movement (UDM), the Africa Muslim Party (AMP) and the Universal Party (UP), and later the now disbanded Independent Democrats (ID), entered into a coalition with the DA, electing its leader at the time, Helen Zille, as the City's Executive Mayor. Other partners in the coalition would also be represented in the multi-party government with positions in the Mayoral Committee.

The 2006 coalition in the City of Cape Town was not without its own challenges, chief of which was the expulsion of the AMP following accusations of conspiracy with the ANC. Although this did not significantly impact on the coalition given the entry of the then very strong Independent Democrats that would ultimately join forces with the DA, it does provide a glimpse into some of the challenges that emerge in coalition governments. Other challenges have been far greater, particularly in the metropolitan municipalities following the 2016 elections. That coalition governments in the metros have been calamitous is fact.

The Nelson Mandela Metropolitan Municipality has seen two Executive Mayors, Athol Trollip of the DA and the late Mongameli Bobani of the UDM, removed from office through votes of no confidence by Council, several administrators, including the City Manager, suspended, and instability that has had a devastating impact on service delivery. The City of Tshwane has also experienced significant instability, rooted in what Professor Mashupye Maserumule refers to in *The Conversation* as a "manifestation of coalition arrangements that serve the partisan interests of parties". The instability led to the resignation of two Mayors – Solly Msimanga in 2019 and Stephens Mokgalapa just a year later. So severe was the instability in the City of Tshwane that the Gauteng Provincial Government opted to place it under administration following the dissolution of the mayoral committee, the resignation of the Mayor and the inability of Council to convene. The coalition in the City of Johannesburg has also been marred by instability. Similar to Tshwane, it was punctuated by the 2019 resignation of the Mayor, Herman Mashaba. This resulted in the reconstitution of the government where the ANC subsequently took the mayorship from the DA through a coalition.

The City of Ekurhuleni has undoubtedly been the most stable of metros under a coalition government. The City has managed to govern successfully with our coalition partners, with limited challenge to stability and the function of government. Unlike other metros where the greatest challenge came from within the coalition itself, our challenge has been facilitated by the opposition through such mechanisms as the sponsoring of motions of no confidence. Although these have failed spectacularly, they do provide a glimpse into how governance works – and the mechanisms that are available to hold government to account. After all, it is the people of South Africa who are the ultimate source of political legitimacy. They alone have the power to determine how we fashion a higher civilisation. And based on historical reference, the civilisation that is being fashioned is one in which coalitions will continue to play a significant role. For this reason, we must invest in theorising them in order that we create a blueprint of how we ought to manage them. At the heart of coalition instabilities in the metros is that there is no theory of governing and therefore no clear strategy on how to govern through a coalition. The greatest danger with this is that we run the risk of constituting coalitions that will inherently implode, because a key element for a successful coalition government is the rationale for its existence. Was it merely to remove the governing party? Are parties working together with the aim of bringing administrative and political stability? And importantly – what did political parties bargain for when the coalitions were formed?

These questions and more are engaged in this book. Through interviews with various local and national government practitioners in the country, as well as the Southern African Development Community (SADC), I have sought to capture the multitude of experiences that have shaped how coalition governments were established, how they worked and, in some cases, how and why they failed. Engagements with practitioners and citizens of the Republic of Zimbabwe demonstrate how coalitions can bring about stability in times of socio-political uncertainty, imploring us to reflect deeply on whether or not the future of a stable South Africa, SADC region and the entirety of the continent, lies in embracing a new imagination of effective party-political systems. As we inch towards the sixth local government elections in democratic South Africa, may we invest ourselves in these reflections.

Mzwandile Masina

Executive Mayor: City of Ekurhuleni

FOREWORD

There comes a time in the life of an organisation when the necessity for self-reflection can no longer be postponed. In the case of former national liberation movements, this time unfortunately comes when an existential crisis has already taken hold. This crisis is characterised by the haemorrhaging of electoral support, a qualitative and quantitative decline in the organisation's membership and internal divisions that tear the organisation asunder. While all former national liberation movements on the African continent have somewhat different contexts, they share important similarities. The first is that they were born from anti-colonial struggles against foreign domination and racial discrimination. The second, linked to the first, is that they are all nationalistic in character, with most of them having dabbled in various ideologies. Some of these movements engaged in armed struggle as a path to independence and democracy, and most of them would ultimately become governing parties in new dispensations. Initially widely supported in the early years of independence, with the passage of time, they would begin to lose their hegemonic power and ultimately, their political support. Numerous scholars have sought to make sense of the factors behind the emergence of this reality which has been noted in all post-independence societies on the African continent. In *Future Realities of Coalition Governments in South Africa*, this discussion is deepened.

Mzwandile Masina, as the African National Congress's Regional Chairperson in the Ekurhuleni Region, is well placed to reflect on the evolving nature of South African people's relationship with the governing party. The Ekurhuleni Region features prominently in our country's liberation struggle history and is a site of historical political conflicts that contributed towards freedom. It was in the region that some of the most brutal struggles were waged including clashes between the ANC and the apartheid government, and between the ANC and the Inkatha Freedom Party. These struggles shaped the socio-political and cultural landscape of the region and is inter-woven in the geohistories of communities and their people. As the Executive Mayor of the City of Ekurhuleni Metropolitan Municipality, and having assumed this position through a coalition government, Masina stands on vantage ground to make reflections on the present and future realities of coalition governments – reflections that are at the centre of this book.

The 2016 municipal elections were a defining point in the polity of South Africa. While there had been coalition governments prior to these elections, it was the first time that the ANC had suffered such widespread electoral defeat, particularly in metropolitan municipalities. Having already lost the City of Cape Town to opposition, the 2016 elections would see the party lose three other metros, namely the City of Johannesburg, the City of Tshwane and Nelson Mandela Bay, to coalitions led by the Democratic Alliance. In the City of Ekurhuleni, the ANC managed to maintain plurality and was positioned to lead the coalition. The ANC lost electoral support in district and local municipalities across the country, mainly in areas that were historically the party's stronghold. And while this may have been troubling, it was important for both the organisation and the people of South Africa, for it set parameters for reflection and dialogue about the future of the country and the ANC's place in it.

With the exception of the City of Ekurhuleni, coalition governments in South Africa's metros and many local municipalities have been characterised by structural and institutional dysfunction. Internal and external divisions have resulted in resignations of mayors and municipal managers, as well as the collapse of Councils. No mayor in the three municipalities that the ANC lost in 2016 has completed their term of office. A simplistic analysis of this reality would draw the conclusion that the ANC alone has the capacity to govern, and that where it does not, instability is inherent. But such an analysis misses the point that the electorate has expressed a resounding vote of no confidence in the ANC. By voting it out of power, they have declared that it is, in fact, incapable of governing and that it cannot be trusted to be the vehicle that will lead South Africa to prosperity. A more reasoned analysis is that coalition governments are a fairly new phenomenon – one not entirely understood in a country whose political milieu has always been defined by a dominant-party system. That no political party was prepared for a coalition government is evidenced by the fact that none had constructed a theoretical blueprint for how these would function. In general the elemental architecture of a coalition government consist of the following:

- How it is put together,
- How it is maintained, and
- How it is dissolved.

And so necessarily, we must ask: in the presence of a coherent blueprint for coalition governments, can they be successful in South Africa and the rest of the region?

Masina attempts to answer this question by posing it to government practitioners, both politicians and administrators, who have been part of coalition governments. The responses are nuanced, but there is clear indication that the seed that coalition governments are a future reality for South Africa has been planted in the minds of political leaders. In the City of Ekurhuleni where the coalition was relatively stable and where the administration has remained intact since its election, there is a sense that with some improvements in aspects like communication, there is great opportunity for a coalition government to be effective. This sentiment is echoed across the country. Curiously and perhaps very importantly, ANC leaders have awakened to this possibility and though their reflections bely discomfort, the fact that the discussion is not outrightly rejected offers hope that the subject can be broached with intelligence, sensibility and the political maturity it demands.

In many ways, *Future Realities of Coalition Governments in South Africa* is a conversation between political leaders and ordinary people – a discourse about the past, present and future of our country. It asks pertinent questions about national liberation movements cum governing parties, and about the entirety of the political life of our country and the African continent. Ultimately, the future of coalition governments will be determined not by political actors, but by the people of South Africa who have fought hard for the right to self-determine. For this reason, they cannot be marginalised from this conversation and through this book, Masina provides a necessary platform for engagement and reflection. It is not a book about how the ANC should reclaim political power, but about how electoral politics are instrumental in fashioning a higher civilisation. And herein lies its strength.

Kgalema Motlanthe

TABLE OF CONTENTS

1

CONTEXTUALISATION OF STATE POWER, ELECTIONS AND COALITION GOVERNMENT

Elections 1

The State as a Power 2

State Power and Party-Political Systems 3

    One-Party System 4

    Two-Party System 5

    Dominant-Party System 5

    Multi-Party System 7

Coalition Government: A Conceptual Discourse 8

Effectiveness and Shortfalls of Coalition Government 9

Origins of Coalition Governments: A Global Context 10

Coalition Government Experiences: An African Context 11

    Coalition Governance in Post-1994 South Africa: Contextualisation 12

    Coalition Governance in Local Government: Contextualisation 13

The 2016 Election Outcomes and Locating the City of Ekurhuleni 14

Gaps in Literature 14

Structure of the Book 15

2

COALITION GOVERNMENTS IN THE SADC REGION: A CASE STUDY OF THE GOVERNMENT OF NATIONAL UNITY IN ZIMBABWE

Zimbabwe and the Government of National Unity 17

    Zimbabwe's History of Conflict 17

    The 2008 Election Violence 19

    The Global Political Agreement 21

Establishing the Government of National Unity 22

Outcomes of the Government of National Unity........................... 23

Analysis of the Primary Data 26

3 THE COALITION EXPERIENCE IN SOUTH AFRICAN LOCAL, DISTRICT AND METROPOLITAN MUNICIPALITIES: 2016 – 2021

The Economy in 2016 29

The Rise in Crime... 30

Popular Protests and Youth Participation 32

A Fractured ANC 35

An Implosion that the Organisation and Experts Saw Coming 38

The Interview Processes 39

Coalition Governments in South Africa: 2016-2021 41

    City of Johannesburg 41

    City of Tshwane... 46

    Nelson Mandela Bay Metropolitan Municipality 52

    Metsimaholo Local Municipality 59

Reflections from Other Political Developments in the Country.............. 62

4 THE COALITION GOVERNMENT IN THE CITY OF EKURHULENI

Election Results 64

The History of Ekurhuleni and Conditions that Led to the ANC's
Decline in Support... 64

Motions of No Confidence 67

The Coalition Experience in the City of Ekurhuleni 68

    The Interview Processes 68

    Coalition Partner One.. 69

    Coalition Partner Two.. 70

    Coalition Partner Three.. 71

Coalition Partner Four 73
Coalition Partner Five 74
Reflections by the Executive Mayor 75
Key Achievements of the Coalition Government in the City of Ekurhuleni 76

Governance 77
Coalition governance 77
Education 78
Service delivery in informal settlements 78
Infrastructure development 79
Support for SMMEs and development of the township economy 80
Land reform 80

5 INTERVIEW WITH MZILIKAZI WA AFRIKA

I am genuinely surprised, Executive Mayor, that you chose a journalist who is not popular in some circles of the African National Congress, to do this interview with 83

Are you saying you are recruiting me into the ANC? 83

Like many South Africans, I am extremely interested in understanding what led to the writing of this book. 83

Some would argue that you have been flirting with the opposition, specifically, the EFF. Is there any truth to this, or do you still believe very strongly in the ruling party? 84

So, neither you nor members of the ANC close to you are considering the formation of a splinter organisation despite some of your public disagreements with what you deem a glacial pace in actualising some of the key resolutions of the 54th National Conference? 85

And yet you have accused ANC Leaders of not implementing conference resolutions 85

Why must the Reserve Bank be nationalised? 86

As someone who is invested in global politics, which have shaped how you make sense of the future of coalition government, I am sure you have studied models of other Reserve Banks in the world. Is your argument in favour of the nationalisation of the central bank congruent with global practice? 87

Prior to the 2016 Local Government elections, you were the Deputy Minister of Trade and Industry. Why did you leave National Government to contest at Local Government? 87

Let's speak about the period leading up to the 2016 Local Government elections. There were indications even before the elections that the ANC was losing its hegemony in many parts of the country. Did you think the party would lose the Metros in Gauteng to the opposition?. 88

How were you feeling as you sat watching the election results coming in from the IEC? 88

At the 54th National Conference in Nasrec, the organisation adopted a unity framework. What necessitated this and is the framework still in place? 88

In the book you speak of the fracture that led to the ANC's loss of power in the 2016 Local Government elections. What contribution as the party's Ekurhuleni Chairperson are you currently making within the structures in helping the ANC heal itself as it still finds itself deeply fractured? 89

In the Metsimaholo Local Municipality in the Free State, the South African Communist Party contested the ANC. There have also been tensions within the alliance over time. Do you think the alliance is still relevant? 90

You were once appointed as the convenor of the ANC Youth League National Task Team. Today the YL is still led through an NTT, with no end in sight. Why is the YL struggling and what are the implications of this for the ANC going towards the 2021 Local Government elections, given the centrality of the youth vote? 91

What kinds of problems? 91

Let's talk coalition governments. The City of Ekurhuleni has undoubtedly been the most stable Metro under a coalition government. What do you think are the ingredients of a successful coalition government? 92

In terms of governance, what has been the highlight for the coalition government in the City of Ekurhuleni? 93

What were the major obstacles in the establishment of the coalition government in Ekurhuleni and how did you deal with them? 93

Who benefits the most in a coalition government and what are those benefits?. 94

Unlike many ANC leaders who have often argued that the ANC needs to reclaim powerfully rather than go into coalitions, you believe that there is a future for them. Does this not place you at odds with your comrades? 94

But don't you think coalition governments pose a significant threat to
governing parties like the ANC? 95

So, you're saying coalitions are inevitable? 95

Problems such as the collapse of government as was the case in the
City of Tshwane? 96

Your research team visited Zimbabwe to gather information about the
Government of National Unity (GNU) that was established in the country
by the MDC and ZANU-PF in 2009. What were some of the surprising
findings that you and your team made on this trip? 96

Does the future of Zimbabwe lie in another GNU? 96

If you ask Mzwandile Masina? 97

Which, in your opinion, is the best model for coalition governments
in the world? 97

Evidence before us suggests that when a coalition government is
unstable as is the case in the City of Tshwane and Nelson Mandela
Bay Metro, it is the citizens who suffer. But what are the rewards
that citizens reap in a stable coalition government like the one
you are leading? 98

What lessons must we learn from the failed coalition governments
in the Metros? 98

You contend that the EFF is not a class enemy of the ANC, but merely its
opposition. Does this mean you believe that the ANC and EFF could
co-govern through a coalition? 99

I doubt that the EFF would want to go into a coalition with the ANC
when it has made it clear throughout its existence that it wants to
remove the party from power, and refused to give it votes that could
have kept the Metros in the hands of the ANC 99

If the City of Ekurhuleni were to be thrust into another coalition
government at the upcoming Local Government elections, would
you enter a coalition with the same partners you are in it with now? 100

Should the OR Tambo School of Leadership that has done significant
intellectual work in teaching members of the ANC around matters of
organisational history, discipline, handling of factionalism, battles of
ideas, etc., consider designing a curriculum on future realities of
coalition governments in South Africa? 100

Would you participate in the drafting of this framework, given your
experience in governing in a coalition? 101

6 REFLECTIONS AND RECOMMENDATIONS

Evolution of National Liberation Movements 102

The Character of South African Political Parties 104

Class Enemies vs Opponent. 107

The Necessity of Coalition Governments 108

CONTEXTUALISATION OF STATE POWER, ELECTIONS AND COALITION GOVERNMENT

To contextualise the study of coalition governments in literature, it is important to conduct a review on existing studies on the topic of multi-party governance. Reflections on the practice of coalition government in relation to origins, and global, continental and domestic contexts as solicited from literature will be covered in this section. From the outset, an attempt is made to elucidate the concept 'coalition government' as this study's primary phenomenon so that the associated contextual discourses can be properly understood. The starting point in engaging the conceptual discourse of coalition governments is to make sense of elections as a mechanism for the attainment of state power.

Elections

Elections are defined as "a formal group decision-making process by which a population chooses an individual or multiple individuals to hold public office" (Encyclopaedia Britannica). In South Africa, elections follow a five-year cycle, with national and provincial elections held simultaneously and municipal elections held two years later. The electoral system is based on party-list proportional representation, which means that parties are represented in proportion to their electoral support. For municipal councils there is a mixed-member system in which wards elect individual councillors alongside those named from party lists. In elections of the National Assembly or parliament, every South African citizen who is 18 or older may vote, including (since the 2014 election) those residing outside South Africa. In elections of a provincial legislature or municipal council, only those residing within the province or municipality may vote. All elections are conducted by the Electoral Commission of South Africa – an election management body established under chapter nine of the South African Constitution.

In South Africa, elections are not only a constitutional mechanism for electing legislators, but are also the foundation on which our liberation struggle was built. It was only in 1994, following decades of a protracted struggle against the draconian apartheid regime, that South Africans of all races could participate in general elections. The elections were also the first held with universal adult suffrage following decades of the exclusion of Black people and other persons of colour, as well as historically, Black men and women without franchise. And while the ANC won 62 percent of the vote, this was shy of the two-thirds majority needed to unilaterally amend the interim constitution, necessitating the formation of a Government of National Unity that would subsequently elect Nelson Rolihlahla Mandela as the country's first democratically elected president.

Elections, evidently, have always been about the contest for state power – the power to control the national assembly, provincial legislatures and municipal councils in order that ideas of the governing party, about how to architect a higher civilisation, could find expression.

The State as a Power

The state is primarily a power. It possesses legal dominion over the population of a definite territory, and its legality is original rather than derived from another power that might dominate it. Other organisations within the state, such as municipalities, are legally the creatures of the state and possess the powers they exercise by delega- tion from the state. The state itself is distinguished by the fact that its powers are not imputed but are native to it. Hence it is the judge of its own legal competence, as well as of the legal competence of the corporations that it creates. The state is the arbiter over both its own legal powers and those of its subjects.

Many measures of state power have been defined in terms of the material capabilities of the state. For example, in the United States "constitutional law, police power is char- acterised as a salient form of state power. This power is defined as the capacity of the states to regulate behaviour and enforce order within their territory for the betterment of the health, safety, morals, and general welfare of their inhabitants" (Encyclopaedia Britannica). This power is exercised by the legislative and executive branches of the various states through the enactment and enforcement of laws.

Italian Marxist philosopher Antonio Gramsci (quoted in Hyug Baeg, 1991) elaborates on this discourse, contending that state power is not only a function of material resources in the conventional sense of the word, but of hegemony. Gramsci contends that ideology plays a significant role in the creation of cultural hegemony, which becomes a means of bolstering the power of the nation-state. Hegemonic power by the state is thus maintained not only through the material image of power that is characterised by coercion and economic or physical force (violence), but also through the projection of consent. However, Snider (1987) argues that there are important differentials in the state's capacity to convert material resources into political power. This thus defines state power within both the global environment and society, based on the twin functions of penetration and extraction.

The traditional conception of the state as primarily a power has been cemented in political philosophy and has been a subject of great debate among historians and scholars. Philosophers such as Hegel have described the state as "the realisation of the ethical ideal" (1967), contending that it is the image and realisation of reason. In his *Philosophy of Right*, Hegel elevates the power of the state to that of God – cementing his idea of its supremacy. The existence of the state, according to Hegel, is essential even when there may be evidence of its defects, for "the state is the actuality of concrete freedom".

German philosopher Karl Marx, and Marxist scholars throughout history, have convincingly challenged this Hegelian perspective of the state as an ethical ideal. In the *Critique of Hegel's Philosophy of Right*, Marx deconstructs the various layers of contradictions in Hegel's submission, at the heart of which is the latter's argument that such instruments as the police and judiciary are spheres of civil society, thus rendering the executive as nothing more than the administration. This failure to recognise the state as a bureaucracy, according to Marx, disregards that "...the bureaucracy according to its essence is the state as formalism, so too it is according to its end. The real end of the state thus appears to the bureaucracy as an end opposed to the state. The mind of the bureaucracy is the formal mind of the state. It therefore makes the formal mind of the state, or the real mindlessness of the state, a categorical imperative. The bureaucracy asserts itself to be the end of the state..."

Whether we employ a Hegelian perspective of the state, and deem it the actuality of concrete freedom, or employ the Marxist perspective that a state is a tool of oppression in the hands of the dominant class, one thing we can agree on as pertains to the state is that it is a powerful instrument with which societies are created and maintained. We can also then agree that elections are an important mechanism for the legitimisation of that instrument. In the contemporary world, elections are and remain the best known and most effective device for connecting citizens to policy makers. They are a formal expression of democratic sovereignty – and of state power. But elections occur within existing party-political systems, and to make sense of how they shape society, we must first understand these systems.

State Power and Party-Political Systems

Having determined that elections are fundamentally a contest for state power, it is necessary that we reflect briefly on the various political party systems in existence. These serve as a measure or indicator of the strength of any nation's democracy. The relationships of political parties in any system give an indication as to the health of its democracy. Where cooperation and consensus are present, there are greater chances that a healthy democracy exists. The opposite is also true: where there is conflict and polarisation, levels of democracy tend to be low or non-existent. Matlosa and Shale (2008) contend that this aspect of a party system is inextricably linked to the prevailing political culture in a country, the ideological orientation of parties, political traditions, and history. In modern democracies, there are four main party systems, namely:

1. One-party system.
2. Two-party system.
3. Dominant-party system.
4. Multi-party system.

One-Party System

In a one-party system, only one political party exists and enjoys a monopoly of power. Other parties, even if they may be in existence, are excluded from contestation for power either by political (*de facto*) or constitutional (*de jure*) means. In situations of a *de facto* one-party system, the ruling party dominates the political landscape and exercises hegemony over all the organs of state. This does not necessarily require the banning of other political parties through a legal or constitutional provision but does mean that only the one party enjoys hegemonic power.

De facto one-party systems have existed throughout history, particularly in post-colonial countries in Africa and Latin America. Examples of these include Lesotho (1970 – 1986), Zimbabwe (1986 – 2000), the Republic of Cuba (1959 – present), Lao People's Democratic Republic (1975 – present), Sahrawi Arab Democratic Republic (1976 – present) and the State of Eritrea (1994 – present), to name but a few. In one-party systems, political pluralism does not exist. The ruling party becomes a permanent government. The party is fused into the state and is enmeshed into the state. The party is thus a metonymy of the state. Inevitably, such a political system is characterised by organs of state being compromised due in large part to lack of accountability. The absence of parliamentary opposition creates fertile ground for various forms of violations, including the violation of obligation that is facilitated by inadequate accountability, non-transparency and impunity.

De jure one-party systems have the same characteristics. In situations of a *de jure* one-party system, the ruling party dominates the political landscape and exercises hegemony over the organs of the state through a deliberate constitutional or legal provision banning the existence of other political parties. This system was particularly pronounced in the 1970s and 1980s on the African continent, where the struggle for independence was marred with fears of collaboration with former superpowers who sought to maintain control of newly politically independent states. Countries that employed a *de jure* one-party system included Angola, Egypt, Senegal, Equatorial Guinea, Malawi, Tanzania,

Zambia, Benin, Mozambique, Burundi, Cameroon, and Côte d'Ivoire, among others. *De jure* one-party systems were also common in Asia and Eastern Europe.

Two-Party System

In a two-party system, also known as a duopoly, two political parties dominate the political system as major parties. The parties both have a roughly equal prospect of winning state power. Conventionally, a two-party system has the following criteria:

1. Although several minor parties may exist, only two parties enjoy sufficient electoral and legislative strength to have a realistic prospect of winning state power.
2. The larger party can govern alone (usually based on legislative majority); the other provides the opposition.
3. Power alternates between these two parties.

The United Kingdom and the United States of America are classical cases of a two-party system wherein two parties, Labour and Conservatives and Democrats and Republicans respectively, dominate the political systems and from time-to-time alternate positions as government and opposition. While some scholars have argued that the two-party system is associated with strong, accountable, and responsive government (Matlosa & Shale, 2008, there has been great criticism of this system. Disch (2002) argues that the two-party system as we know it dates only to the twentieth century and that it thwarts democracy by wasting the votes and silencing the voices of dissenters. She terms this system a "tyranny". Jackson Nudelman (2020) echoes these sentiments, arguing that "from a comprehensive standpoint, our system leaves no room for the representation of 'radical' third party voters and their fundamental beliefs which refuse to concede to either of the two major parties' platforms". Two-party systems have also been criticised for encouraging adversarial politics, ideological polarisation and emphasis on conflict and confrontation rather than consensus, persuasion, and compromise.

Dominant-Party System

A dominant-party system is one where only one party exercises hegemony as the governing or ruling party over a long period of time under conditions of fragmented, disjointed and enfeebled opposition parties. Unlike the one-party system, a dominant-party system is competitive in that several parties compete for power in regular elections even if the electoral contest is dominated by a single major party. Such a party enjoys a prolonged control of state power, enjoys a monopoly of policymaking, and faces a weak opposition with slim prospects for capturing state power in the foreseeable future.

One of the prominent features of the dominant-party system is the tendency for faction fighting and internal conflicts within the dominant party. While the dominant-party system, in and of itself, does not negate democracy and political stability, it has been criticised on a number of grounds, including the following:

1. A dominant-party system may erode the constitutional distinction between state and party in power.
2. A dominant-party system may undermine the checks and balances and the effectiveness of parliament as a watchdog over the executive organ of the state.
3. Prolonged control of state power could engender complacency, arrogance, and corruption in the dominant ruling party (with scandals involving allegations of corruption).
4. A dominant-party system is characterised by a weak and ineffective opposition whose criticism and protests are often ignored by the dominant party.
5. The exercise of a 'semi-permanent' party of government in the form of a dominant party may corrode the democratic spirit by encouraging the electorate to fear change and to stick with the 'natural' party of government (Matlosa & Shale, 2008:12).

Various countries in the world have experienced the dominant-party system. These include India, Japan, Botswana and Namibia, to name but a few. In Japan, the Liberal Democratic Party was in power from 1955 until it was dislodged in 1993, and while it continues to enjoy relative hegemony, it is now compelled to enter coalitions with smaller parties to maintain its hold on power. Following its attainment of independence in 1947, India was ruled by the Congress Party of India – a run it maintained for three decades. The Botswana Democratic Party, founded in 1961, has been the governing party since Botswana gained independence from Britain in 1966. Until recently, the African National Congress enjoyed hegemony in South Africa, winning national and local government elections with an outright majority. In two instances, the party won a two-thirds majority – a clear indicator of its electoral strength.

The argument that dominant-party systems are characterised by internal conflict and factionalism within the party holds true. A vivid example of this can be gleaned in Botswana where, in the recent 2019 general elections to elect members of parliament and local government councillors, there was a significant split in the Botswana Democratic Party, with the former president, Ian Khama, leaving the party and switching his support to the opposition Botswana Patriotic Front. A similar situation occurred in South Africa where in 2008, the African National Congress saw one of its most devastating splits with the formation of the Congress of the People. The party was founded by former ANC members Mosiuoa Lekota, Mbhazima Shilowa and Mluleki George to contest the 2009 general election. The party would go on to receive over a million votes, translating to more than a seven percent share of the vote and thirty seats in the national assembly. These intense factional battles characterise governing parties in dominant-party systems, but evidence suggests that parties formed out of these tensions and splits do not necessarily become stronger in the long-run.

Multi-Party System

A multi-party system is marked by competition among more than two political parties. Under this system many parties exist with equal chances to become the governing party, either individually or through coalitions. The major defining features of a multi-party system are party coalitions within and outside parliament and coalition governments. For instance, in Germany's multi-party system, the two major parties, namely, the Social Democratic Party and the Christian Democratic Union, have governed the country through political coalitions that also involve smaller parties. Multi-party coalition governments in Germany are historical, with the Weimer Republic, the German state from 1918 to 1933, having been comprised of a coalition between the Social Democratic Party, the Christian Centre Party, as well as the German Democratic Party and the People's Party, both of which were of liberal persuasion (Williamson, 1982). Conventionally, coalition politics are associated with proportional representation (PR) and mixed electoral systems.

The main strength of multiparty systems is that they create internal checks and balances within government and exhibit a bias in favour of debate, conciliation and compromise. The main criticism of the multi-party system relates to the pitfalls of formation, maintenance and sustenance of coalitions both inside and outside government. Coalition governments may be fractured and unstable (as we witnessed in the metros). In the SADC region, the only country with a multiparty system is Mauritius. The tradition of party coalitions in Mauritius both inside and outside government has not generated political instability or threatened the country's liberal democracy.

Understanding these different party-political systems aids us to better situate the future we envisage. But more than this, it provides us with an important theoretical basis for why the multi-party system could possibly be the best option for our maturing democracy. There is evidence, as will be demonstrated in the next chapter, that democracies work best in party-political systems that make allowance for greater representation and a multiplicity of voices, provided that these all converge on the issue of genuine nation-building and auto-centric development. The converse is also true: that understanding different party-political systems also provides us with an appreciation of why so many democracies have failed.

Empirical evidence demonstrating the salient pitfalls of one-party states is abundant. While the rationale for this particular party-political system in Africa, Latin America and Asia has been the need to advance the post-independence struggle that has often been sabotaged and compromised by retreating colonial powers, as has been contended by various national liberation and revolutionary movements, the reality is that the long-term costs of sustaining such a political system have far outweighed the benefits. Often, one-party states created at the dawn of independence have been instituted through the militarisation of the state. Cervenka (1987) gives a detailed analysis of the effects of militarisation of Africa on human rights. He argues, importantly, that militarisation need not refer only to rule by the gun or to military conflicts, but can, broadly, refer to the usurpation of political power by soldiers through military coups (as was the case in Zimbabwe), armed conflicts and the importation of arms by which wars are perpetuated, and the arms build-up and military expenditure. In such environments of militarisation, human rights are sacrificed, leading to great instability and the threat to the very legitimacy of governments.

Two-party states such as the United States of America and the United Kingdom have also proven to have a great degree of political polarisation that makes it extremely difficult for a multiplicity of voices to find expression. It is for this reason that the kind of government that South Africa needs to have, if it is to actualise its ideal of the realisation of a National Democratic Society characterised by a spirit of unity in diversity, is a multi-party-political system where coalitions govern. Therefore, this system must be given close study.

Coalition Government: A Conceptual Discourse

The reviewed literature demonstrates a great deal of similarities even in texts used in the definition of the concept "coalition government". It is defined by Kadima (2014, quoted in Booysen, 2014:67) as "the association of at least two political parties, working together in Parliament and/or government on the basis of election outcomes". Coalition governance usually occurs in cases where no single political party attains majority votes from the election results thereby opting to combine votes to form a government. The main objective behind a coalition of political parties as asserted by Karume (2003, cited in Ogunnubi, Shai & Mokgosi, 2017:41) is to control the executive. It is about the contest of state power. Thus, it is through the control of executive office that political parties form a cabinet and enforce desired policies in the polity. South Africa's road to democracy evidences the significance of the attainment of state power. The electoral agenda of the ANC towards 1994 was not only the assumption of political office, but it was also the attainment of state power in order to introduce policies that would take South Africa out of the heinous depths of the apartheid dispensation into a democracy. Coalition governments, in the context of South Africa with its amoral past, serve not only to claim state power, but to right a historical wrong.

However, Botha (2004) argues that a coalition government must not be seen as completely different from a one-party government that is characterised by authoritarianism. The author argues that both systems (single-party dominance or party coalition government) are principally conditioned by the nature of the political system adopted country-wide. South Africa's democracy, for example, is a multi-party democracy that allows single-party dominance or coalition government based on election results. Put differently, these two methods of governance may vary in their *modus operandi,* but their effectiveness is strictly dependent on the nature of the political system adopted. Therefore, this discussion is critical for this study in that it raises a scholarly quest for the need to understand the associated advantages and disadvantages for parties that opt for coalition government.

Effectiveness and Shortfalls of Coalition Government

Conducted studies such as Kadima (2006), McMillan (2014) and the National Democratic Institute (NDI, 2017) found that coalition governments have now become a global practice. As such, coalition government as a practice increases the political competition required for strengthening governments. However, while this is the main argument for adherents to the multi-party government system, there are other critical outcomes of coalitions that demand greater analysis. One of them, according to Kadima, is that such party-political systems can foster national unity and cohesion. Kadima, in his seminal study, argues that the Labour Party (LP) and its historical rival, the Parti Mauricien Socialiste Democrate (PMSD) of Mauritius used coalition governance to achieve national cohesion.

The general election of 1967 in Mauritius was bitterly fought along ethnic considerations. The Hindu majority massively supported political independence while the minorities, fearing political domination by the Hindus, voted overwhelmingly against Independence and in favour of political integration/association with the United Kingdom. The Independence Party, which comprised three political formations, won 56 percent of the votes while the anti-independence bloc captured a significant 44 percent. The country was deeply divided and there was an absolute necessity to heal these wounds. Two years later, the coalition government that won the elections collapsed and a new one, of the main party that fought for independence (Labour Party) and the one that opposed it (PMSD), was sworn in. It was hailed as a path-breaking move to build bridges between the two camps, to prevent political alienation, to encourage broad-based participation in the running of the country, to nurture the newly born nation and to avoid a descent into instability and socio-political crisis. It was a power-sharing strategy that allowed the country to get on with the task of nation building and economic development rather than be engulfed in acrimonious ethnic rivalry. It worked well for years and delivered socio-economic progress to the country (Sithanen, 2003).

Another important case in which a coalition government served to foster national unity is that of Rwanda, which in 1994 endured one of the worst ethnic genocides the African continent has ever experienced. The Rwanda genocide, anchored on the rivalries of the Hutu and Tutsi ethnic groups, saw the massacre of nearly one million people – mostly of the Tutsi minority. By the time the Tutsi-led Rwandese Patriotic Front (RPF) gained control of the country through a military offensive in early July, just three months after the beginning of the genocide, hundreds of thousands of Rwandans were dead and two million refugees, mainly Hutus, had fled Rwanda, exacerbating what had already become a full-blown humanitarian crisis. After its victory, the RPF established a coalition government similar to that agreed upon at Arusha in Tanzania, with Pasteur Bizimungu, a Hutu, as president and Paul Kagame, a Tutsi, as vice president and Minister of Defence. The lasting result of this coalition is that Rwanda is today one of the most stable and economically developed countries on the continent (World Bank, 2021).

These are but two critical cases for benchmarking effective coalitions. In the next chapter, we will look at Zimbabwe as a case study, to analyse how coalition governments can serve as instruments for redress. Doherty (2004) argues that coalition governments can be effective, but they must first and foremost be beneficial to all their constituents, and have a willingness to compromise and establish a sense of partnership regard-less of the size of the party. As in the case of Mauritius and Rwanda, where the RPF was comprised in great part of an ethnic minority, where there is a sense of common purpose, the size of the party is negligible, and is subordinated to the national interest and common good of and for the people.

But the literature also demonstrates that coalition governments are not without critics. Müller and Miller (2005:12) and McMillan (2014:202) point out that this practice is relent-lessly prone to chaos and could lead to instabilities if not managed well. They contend that because of the need to obtain ratification from the involved parties within the coali-tion, decisions and actions may take longer than expected, resulting in service delivery protests and lack of policy implementation. The criticism is legitimate, as evidenced in the coalition catastrophe in the City of Tshwane, the City of Johannesburg, and Nelson Mandela Metropolitan Municipality. The instabilities wrought by the collapse of coalitions in the said metros demonstrates that in the absence of cohesion, this party-political system can prove calamitous for ordinary citizens who are on the receiving end of lack of service delivery emanating from the instabilities and chaos.

Origins of Coalition Governments: A Global Context

There is a consensus among public administration scholars such as Oyugi (2006), Kadima and Lembani (2006), Kadima (2014) and Maserumule, Mokati and Vil-Nkomo (2016) that the notion of coalition governments has its roots in Western European countries. Indeed, it was found that by December 2011 almost two-thirds of the countries affiliated to the European Union (EU) were facilitated through coalition governments (Maserumule *et al.*, 2016). These include Germany, Belgium, Italy, Austria, Israel, the Netherlands, and Scandinavian countries in general.

Germany, for example, is currently governed through a coalition led by the Christian Democratic Union and Social Democrats. This came about because of recurring political crises since the period 1966 to 1969, which led to the formation of the coalition government. Critical to the German experience and Europe in general is the sustained unity between the involved parties in the legislature or executive. Therefore, unity as feature of coalitions is important and could be used to improve the coalition councils' [hung councils'] crises, as recently seen in some parts of South Africa's Gauteng local government (see Maserumule *et al.*, 2016).

In addition, there are countries other than in Europe that have a long history of coalition governments, India being a prime example. The 1989 national elections saw India governed through coalitions. Before this, in 1950 when India, under the Indian National Congress (INC), faced economic instability, it entered into a coalition government with the erstwhile State of Travancore-Chochi (Chander, 2004). Whereas it is worth understanding that the lessons above are relevant for benchmarking, it is equally important to note that none of these countries have produced a blue-print for the success of a coalition government (Kadima, 2014), meaning that this practice is not a one-size-fit all. An attempt will be made in this study to explore reasons for this and subsequently, to make a case for how South Africa can design its own coalition government blueprint.

Coalition Government Experiences: An African Context

The practice of coalition governments is relatively new in the African polity. This is at the heart of why the literature on this subject is significantly limited. Kadima and Lembani (2006), in their book *The Politics of Party Coalitions in Africa*, concurs with the above view, arguing that one of the reasons the phenomenon was not largely researched in Africa is because the majority of African scholars did not see value in studying coalitions. In addition, the few studies conducted in Africa show that most African countries began embracing the notion of a coalition governance after decades of independence, at a point where former national liberation movements begin to haemorrhage electoral support. Kenya, for example, attained independence in 1963 and introduced a multi-party politics in 1992, then only reintroduced this later in 2007 after the fiercely contested presidential election that was characterised by post-election violence and instability. Other countries on the continent, including Zimbabwe, which is studied in detail in the next chapter, also resorted to coalition governments following fierce electoral contestation and contested election results. And although there is evidence that such a compromise has brought about a great degree of stability in many cases, it is not an ideal circumstance.

In Malawi, Kadima and Lembani (2006) conducted a study that examined the state of coalitions and they argued that, to some extent, that coalitions can negate the question of ideological concentration especially when the involved parties share a common and immediate agenda. According to these authors, the formed coalition named "Mgwrizano" carried a single agenda, which was to unseat the incumbent United Democratic Front (UDF) from office. Regrettably, this objective lacked ideological affinity thereby putting the future of the coalition at risk. It can be argued that at the heart of the failure of coalitions established in the metros in South Africa following the 2016 municipal election has been precisely this lack of ideological convergence. In Chapter three, experiences from practitioners who were instrumental in these coalitions are explored.

This is one but most critical feature of coalition governments that ought to be considered in studying the system discourse. In addition, Kapa and Shale's (2014) study looked into the consequences for the party system, democratic consolidation, national cohesion and state governability of party coalitions and alliances from the period 2007 to 2012 in Lesotho. These authors have correctly established that governance under coalition can be extremely difficult at times and this is often caused by the varying political and ideological orientations of the parties involved. This observation is corroborated by Booysen (2014) who, using South Africa as a case study, argued that at a party level it seems unambiguous to forge coalitions, yet it remains difficult when in government because a slight disagreement between the parties might collapse the union. This study therefore will expose the salient realities emanating from multi-party coalitions that inform coalition councils in South Africa, with the City of Ekurhuleni as an important focal point for reference.

Coalition Governance in Post-1994 South Africa: Contextualisation

As indicated, the notion of multi-party governance or coalition governance does not have origins in Africa. South Africa, like many other contemporary democratic states on the African continent, has adopted the theory and practice of coalition governments, which is ostensibly replacing the one-party system of the polity since the 1994 transitions (see Kotze, 2016; Independent Electoral Commission of South Africa (IEC), 2016). The 1994 general elections resulted in radical transitions that incepted a democratic government led by the ANC and effectively replaced the National Party-led apartheid government. With its arrangement of government (national, provincial, and local spheres) as described in section 40 of the Constitution (1996), South Africa has had six national and provincial elections coupled with five local governments since 1994. There has never been a coalition government in both national and provincial government as the ANC continued with its dominance over national government with eight the nine provinces, except the Western Cape, since 1994. This is precisely what makes the 2016 local government elections so critical for study.

Unarguably, the ANC as a political and governing party had not anticipated the possibility of losing power as spectacularly as it did in the 2016 elections. While there were some internal concerns about the road to these elections, punctuated in particular by the simmering tensions in the City of Tshwane and Nelson Mandela Bay (NMB) (these are elaborated on in Chapter three), the idea that we would be unseated from office never cemented itself in our collective imagination. But the outcome certainly introduced to the organisation the very real idea of a future without historical dominance – a future in which coalition governance must be at the centre of discourse and political strategy.

Coalition Governance in Local Government: Contextualisation

Existing literature that has been analysed shows divisions among South African researchers on the emergence of coalitions in local politics. Engel (2016) and Greffrath and Van der Waldt (2016) found that South Africa's local government has been susceptible to the practice of multi-party governance. Therefore, in as early as 2018, Moshodi conducted a study on *Coalition politics in the new political landscape in South Africa*, strongly acknowledging the 2016 local government elections as a turning point in the political history of elections whereby all political parties, with the incumbent ANC included, failed to attain 50 plus 1 percent of the votes in four metropolitan municipalities, namely, Johannesburg, Tshwane, Ekurhuleni, and NMB, necessitating party coalitions. This study was significant because it highlighted the character and challenges facing NMB, the City of Tshwane and Johannesburg, respectively. Despite Ekurhuleni's case being omitted, Moshodi's (2018:27) findings appear to suggest that coalitions in local politics only began in 2016. The same suggestion is observed in Mokgosi, Shai and Ogunnubi (2017) in their article 'Local Government Coalition in Gauteng Province of South Africa: Challenges and Opportunities'. This finding is at odds with the historic events of coalitions in the local sphere. Ndletyana (2018), in the article *Coalitions councils: Origins, composition and impact on local governance* concurs, arguing that the notion of coalition government in South African local politics is as old as the new local government system that was introduced in 2000. Using 2000–2016 IEC data, he further reveals that:

> Before 2016 local elections, local government had experienced a total of 97 coalition municipalities. The 2016 elections pushed that tally up to 124. They were highest in 2011 at 37, followed by the 2006 elections at 31. The 2016 elections, despite their prominence, actually produced the lowest number of coalition councils thus far, at 27. (Ndletyana, 2019:139).

Ndletyana is certainly correct in his argument. And as I have already asserted in the Introduction, coalitions are not a new phenomenon in South African politics. But the 2016 elections did mark a significant turning point not only because they marked the first time that the ANC was unseated from strategic metropolitan municipalities so spectacularly, but because the coalitions that followed presented unprecedented challenges for local government that would ultimately expose the glaring weaknesses of the governance framework in municipalities. This is elaborated upon in Chapter three.

The 2016 Election Outcomes and Locating the City of Ekurhuleni

It is clear from the foregoing that the revised literature is agreed that nascent from the coalition governments in South African metropolitan municipalities is the 2016 elections, the outcomes of which included the eight metros. Results also indicate that in no Gauteng metros was there an outright majority. This was reflective of the failure of the ANC as the governing party to sustain its historical political dominance through elections. It represented political dynamics and new trends in the political divide in South Africa. Notably, one critical aspect raised in Engel (2016), Masipa (2017) and Moshodi (2018) studies, which is going to be dealt with in this study, is the need for coalition councils to forge a strong cooperative front when it comes to service delivery.

The City of Ekurhuleni is governed by a coalition council. Following the 2016 local government elections, the ANC maintained plurality, winning 48.44 percent of the votes, with the DA obtaining 34. 13 percent and the EFF 11.10 percent. This led to a hung council and subsequently necessitated a coalition. Evidence indicates that the coalition established in the City of Ekurhuleni in 2016 has been the most stable of all metropolitan municipalities in South Africa. Where all other coalitions, namely, the City of Tshwane, the City of Johannesburg and Nelson Mandela Bay Metropolitan Municipality have at various points collapsed, with the City of Tshwane at some point being placed under administration, Nelson Mandela Bay changing mayors several times following the ousting of sitting mayors, and the City of Johannesburg seeing a mayor resign, the City of Ekurhuleni maintained the same political administration led by the same Executive Mayor from 2016 to the end of term in 2021. And while the City did not experience the catastrophic challenges that characterised other metros, it did experience its own fair share of difficulties, including two motions of no confidence against the Executive Mayor, brought on by the opposition. The coalition was not without its own difficulties, even though these were resolved efficiently. Despite this, the City of Ekurhuleni has many important lessons to share with the country about coalition governments – their strengths, weaknesses, opportunities, and threats. Whether its working model can be transposed to other local, district and metropolitan municipalities is a discussion that this book will hopefully spark.

Gaps in Literature

Hardly any perused literature on the continent addresses with deep reflection the current and future realities of coalition governments in the local sphere of government. The same could be said about the blueprint attesting to successful coalition government within the global context, as previously argued by Kadima (2014). As such, Ndletyana (2018:141), Booysen (2014) and Botha (2004) are in agreement that the emergence of coalition governments within South African local government, with its causes and impacts, has been under-researched. Therefore, this presents a gap in the literature that this book is going to explore with a special focus on the current and future realties of multi-party governance. Being the Executive Mayor in the City of Ekurhuleni, the only metropolitan municipality that has maintained relative stability under a coalition government, privileges me to provide meaningful reflections on the current realities and experiences of coalition governments. This will further assist in harnessing the conceptualisations and contexts derived herein to shape future discourse analysis on the selected case studies.

Structure of the Book

Following this chapter on the contextualisation of state power, elections and coalition government, which sought to locate the discussion on coalition governments in academic literature, the following chapter will analyse the coalition experiences in the SADC region, with a case study of Zimbabwe. The aim of this chapter is to understand the historical basis and political conditions that led to the Global Political Agreement (GPA), and to understand how the coalition government in the form of the Government of National Unity (GNU) was experienced by both the political parties involved as well as ordinary citizens in the country and the diaspora. The third chapter of the book analyses the coalition experience in local, district and metropolitan municipalities in South Africa in the 2016–2021 period, with a specific focus on the four metros that went into coalitions for the first time in this election, namely, the City of Johannesburg, City of Tshwane, Nelson Mandela Bay Metropolitan Municipality and the City of Ekurhuleni. Chapter four is a comprehensive analysis of the coalition in the City of Ekurhuleni, focusing mainly on the experiences of coalition partners and their perspectives on the future of coalition governments in South Africa and beyond. Chapter five is a comprehensive interview between myself, in my capacity as the Executive Mayor of the City of Ekurhuleni, and award-winning journalist Mzilikazi Wa Afrika, on the state of the coalition in the City of Ekurhuleni, the lessons learned and the future realities of coalition governments in South Africa. The final chapter provides a summary of the discussions and arguments contained in the book and attempts to give some recommendations as to how coalition governments can be made to work for the benefit of the electorate. Importantly, it assesses global best practice with our own local experiences to lay the foundation for what could be a blueprint to establishing coalitions that work.

COALITION GOVERNMENTS IN THE SADC REGION: A CASE STUDY OF THE GOVERNMENT OF NATIONAL UNITY IN ZIMBABWE

The nature and fate of coalition governments on the African continent is evidence of the fact that the very idea of such governments is new in the African polity. At the heart of some of the failures of coalition governments on the continent is the lack of a substantial blueprint that could guide the ideological and pragmatic approach to how such governments ought to be constructed and consolidated. Kadima (2006) makes the contention that one of the reasons the phenomenon has not been given greater attention by African scholars is that many of them do not see value in studying coalitions, in part due to the hegemonic power that has historically been wielded by former national liberation movements turned governing parties. In the limited instances where studies on coalition governments have been conducted, it has largely been at a point where these former national liberation movements have begun to haemorrhage electoral support and to have their very legitimacy challenged by citizens, as was the case with the formation of the Government of National Unity in Zimbabwe. The implication of such an approach is that coalition governments are largely studied post-mortem. And while this is important in so far as providing reflections on how these governments were constituted, the observations of those who were part of them and the citizenry that experienced them, as well as their overall effectiveness, it often pays little attention to the theoretical orientations of these governments.

These orientations matter because it is in understanding them that we can make sense of how effective and sustainable coalition governments can be built. This will go a long way in mitigating the circumstances that resulted in the collapse of nearly all coalition governments in South African metropolitan municipalities following the 2016 local government elections, and the seeming unsustainability of governments of national unity within the Southern Africa Development Community (SADC) region. But in setting parameters for this approach, it remains necessary to study the histories of coalition governments in the region, both in terms of the conditions that gave rise to them and their effectiveness in service delivery and other important objectives of government.

Zimbabwe and the Government of National Unity

Making sense of the legacy of the Government of National Unity (GNU) in Zimbabwe is a complex exercise that demands more than a simple study of the literature that has been generated by scholars and practitioners who were involved in the implementation of this government. It is an exercise that also demands conversation with ordinary Zimbabwean people who were the biggest stakeholders in this GNU. For this reason, it was necessary to visit the country to engage not only the key political players who were part of the GNU process, but with ordinary people whose experiences of it matter more. Some of these experiences are captured in this chapter and reflect the profound ways in which the re-imagination of forms of government has the potential to bring about stability and rebuild trust in the very institution of government that in many parts of the region, including South Africa, is experiencing a serious trust deficit. To understand the GNU in Zimbabwe, it is important to reflect briefly on the historical material conditions that set parameters for its existence and necessity.

Zimbabwe's History of Conflict

The GNU in Zimbabwe was established in 2009 based on the Global Political Agreement (GPA), a power-sharing agreement that closed a chapter on years of political instability and conflict between the ruling Zimbabwe African National Union – Patriotic Front (ZANU-PF) and the Movement for Democratic Change (MDC), the main opposition party in Zimbabwe. For nearly a decade, ZANU-PF and the MDC had a relationship characterised by violent political rivalry. In response to the growing support that the MDC was receiving largely from civil society activists, the trade union and labour movement, intellectuals and the urban population, ZANU-PF responded by unleashing a campaign of dispensing violence against opposition. Mutisi (2011) contends that the cardinal factors that contributed to this conflict were ideological posture, power, governance, and resource distribution. But beyond the unstable political environment that this rivalry created, it also had devastating socio-economic consequences for Zimbabwe. It resulted in "increased rates of unemployment, growing levels of poverty and declining life expectancy rates affecting the populace" (Mutisi, 2011:2) and set parameters for other forms of systematic violence as well as the erosion of the legitimacy of democratic institutions that became entangled in the conflict.

That the conflict between the ZANU-PF and the MDC was ideological is evidenced in the language that the two parties used in characterising each other. The latter had always described the MDC as a "puppet of the West". In a rally televised by state media back in June 2003, the late former president, Robert Mugabe, reacting to the arrest of late MDC leader Morgan Tsvangirai, stated that "The puppet of the West deserves jail time" (*Independent News*, 2003). It had always been a contention of the ZANU-PF that the leading opposition party was a surrogate of Britain tasked with orchestrating a regime-change agenda that sought to undermine the legitimacy of the government and broadly, the state. The MDC, on the other hand, has always maintained the stance that the socio-political and economic challenges that confront Zimbabwe were the direct result of disastrous policy choices by the ruling ZANU-PF. These policies, the MDC argues, have led to economic ruin that has seen millions of Zimbabweans rendered indigent and millions more flee to the diaspora in search of better economic opportunities and social stability.

An analysis into post-independence politics on the African continent indicates that the language used by ZANU-PF is commonly used by former national liberation movements turned governing parties in the characterisation of opposition parties and increasingly, civil society movements. Admittedly, the ANC has on many occasions employed this language in describing opposition parties and has defined as the work of a "third force" legitimate popular struggles that have sought to challenge government on various human rights and service delivery issues. That such language is deeply problematic is not conjecture. In the case of Zimbabwe, it has been the foundation on which arbitrary arrests of opposition and civil society leaders, state-sanctioned violence and political unrest have been built. It may be argued that one of the worst genocides that the African continent has ever witnessed, Gukurahundi, was fuelled by this language. Such an argument would not be incorrect.

Gukurahundi refers to a genocide that was waged by the Zimbabwe National Army (ZNA) from early 1983 to 1987. Zimbabweans, predominantly of Ndebele descent in the Matabeleland and Midlands provinces, most of whom were supporters of the ZANU-PF rival, Zimbabwe African People's Union (ZAPU), were targets of vicious systematic massacres (Murambadoro, 2015). Empirical evidence provided by various historians and scholars suggests that at the heart of the Gukurahundi genocide was the pursuit of political objectives whose main purpose was the decimation of opposition that was seen as posing an impediment to the ideals of the recently won independence. Zimbabwe had gained its independence in 1980 – just three years before the genocide occurred.

The decimation of dissent during Gukurahundi was not, as the narrative on the part of the ZANU-PF suggests, simply to protect the gains of the revolution that were supposedly under threat from ZAPU with the aid of ordinary people in Matabeleland. This argument is incongruent with historical fact. For one thing, ZAPU was a Socialist party aligned with the Soviet Union. Dumiso Dabengwa, who served as the head of intelligence in the Zimbabwe People's Revolutionary Army (ZIPRA), the armed wing of ZAPU, during the Rhodesian Bush War (also known as the Second Chimurenga), explores the extent of the relations between ZAPU and the Union of the Soviet Socialist Republics (USSR) in a journal paper titled "Relations between ZAPU and the USSR, 1960s–1970s: A personal view" (2017). In the same issue, Vladimir Shubin, who served as Secretary of the Soviet Afro-Asian Solidarity Committee and Head of the Africa Section of the

Communist Party of the Soviet Union (CPSU) International Department, also offers extensive analysis of this strong relationship. The idea that ZAPU posed a threat to the revolution is not in alignment with a movement committed to the ideals of Socialism and people's power. Furthermore, ZAPU was instrumental in the fight against the White minority Smithian regime. ZANU and ZAPU both fought the Rhodesian government in the Second Chimurenga. Its commitment to the pursuit of freedom for Zimbabwean people can thus not be subjected to erasure.

What has become clear with the study of history, as detailed extensively by historian Dr Stuart Doran (2017), is that at the heart of the Gukurahundi genocide was an attempt on the part of ZANU to establish a one-party state. In Chapter one, this party-political system is defined as one wherein only one political party exists and enjoys a monopoly of power. Other parties, even if they may be in existence, are excluded from contestation for power either by political (*de facto*) or constitutional (*de jure*) means. This history is embedded in the contemporary struggles of Zimbabwe, and in part of the violence that characterised the Zimbabwean polity leading to the Global Political Agreement established in 2009. University of Zimbabwe Political Science professor Lloyd Sachikonye (2011) makes the profoundly important argument that the contemporary violence that we see in Zimbabwe today is the product of decades of institutionalised violence in the country, which began with the violent actions of the Rhodesian armed forces and inter-party conflicts that occurred in the Second Chimurenga. He contends that the post-2000 migration patterns in Zimbabwe "cannot simply be explained in terms of the search for greener economic pastures. Escape from authoritarianism, violence, trauma, and fear is a large factor behind the exodus" (Sachikonye, 2011). It is instructive that this book was published shortly after the establishment of the GNU, for the political climate that had led Zimbabwe to the power-sharing deal was one defined by the violence, trauma, and fear which Sachikonye is referring to.

The 2008 Election Violence

The 2008 general elections in Zimbabwe were without doubt the most violent and deadly that the country has seen. The synchronised presidential, parliamentary, senatorial, and local elections were held in March 2008 in an environment of political tensions and extreme economic difficulties. Opposition parties had raised concerns about the handling of the political process, which they contended was designed to use a margin of terror to facilitate a ZANU-PF victory. Similar observations were made by human rights and civil society groups, including Amnesty International and Human Rights Watch (HRW), who warned that the political climate that had been created would not enable free, fair and democratic elections. In March 2008, HRW released a report titled *All Over Again: Human Rights Abuses and Flawed Electoral Conditions in Zimbabwe's Coming General Elections* in which it argued that the climate of repression and intimidation, as well as electoral flaws, made free and fair elections impossible. Nonetheless, the elections went ahead, but for more than a month, the results were not released by the Zimbabwe Electoral Commission (ZEC), sparking concerns that systematic rigging was underway. The MDC approached the courts for intervention, to no avail. Two months after the elections, the ZEC announced that MDC leader Morgan Tsvangirai had won most of the votes, at 47.9 percent against incumbent president Robert Mugabe's 43.2 percent. Because neither of the two presidential candidates had won an outright majority, this necessitated a second round of voting to determine an outright winner. A run-off was scheduled for the following month, and even though the MDC maintained that Tsvangirai had won, the party agreed to participate in the second round.

The weeks leading up to the second round of elections was marked by unprecedented violence. A 2008 report by Human Rights Watch, titled *Bullets for each of you: State-sponsored violence since Zimbabwe's March 29 elections,* captures the state-sponsored violence that was happening across the country, focusing on patterns of violence that included killings, abductions, beatings, lootings, and destruction of property, as well as arbitrary arrests of opposition activists and academics. The Zimbabwe Lawyers for Human Rights (ZLHR), in a statement released during this period, explained the arrests as follows: "Since 14 April 2008, at least 150 people have been arrested and are currently detained in custody at Harare Central police station alone. The recent arrests and continuing violations of fundamental rights and freedoms have been exacerbated by state actors who are working hand-in-hand with the ruling ZANU-PF party militia to unleash their coercive apparatus on an innocent electorate. This campaign of terror has been widespread across the country and is being perpetrated against any person who is suspected to have cast their vote against the ruling party, as well as their families" (ZLHR, 2008).

The HRW report contends, as does Sachikonye (2011), that while violence was being meted out on both sides of the political divide, it was the ruling party that had a monopoly on this violence as it used state institutions and instruments to facilitate the violence, and that the opposition was responding to what had become an untenable and fatal situation. Various reports and studies including by the Electoral Institute for Sustainable Democracy in Africa (2008), HRW (2008), Ploch (2010) and Cuneo et al. (2017) posited that the violence extended to the denial to healthcare access for opposition activists and sympathisers, who were turned away from public hospitals. The Zimbabwe Association of Doctors for Human Rights indicated at the time that the number of victims of violence and torture documented by members of the association was on the increase, with nearly three hundred victims being treated in just one month (ZADHR, 2008). In addition to this, police raided Harvest House, the MDC headquarters in Harare, as well as the offices of the Zimbabwe Elections Support Network, and arrested hundreds of people, some of whom would later be tortured and beaten.

The explosive violence in the country resulted in Tsvangirai withdrawing from the race, arguing that the election was undemocratic, and a violent sham designed to punish MDC voters. This was corroborated by the HRW report that stated: "The violence has been particularly concentrated in former rural strongholds of the Zimbabwe African National Union-Patriotic Front (ZANU-PF)-areas that to the party's shock voted for the MDC in the parliamentary and first-round presidential elections. Punishing "sell-outs," former ZANU-PF supporters who voted for the MDC, is a clear objective. Within government-supporting circles, the operation has been dubbed *"Operation Makavhoterapapi?"* (Operation Where Did You Put Your Vote?)" (Human Rights Watch, 2008). With Tsvangirai out of the race, President Mugabe went on to win the election by a huge margin of 85.5 percent, with an increase of more than one million votes from the first round just a month earlier. He was sworn in as the president of Zimbabwe. But despite having "won" the presidential election, the ZANU-PF lost its majority in parliament, with the two MDC factions winning a combined 51.27 percent of the vote against ZANU-PF's 45.94 percent.

The Global Political Agreement

Following the elections, former South African president Thabo Mbeki was tasked with facilitating a political solution that would ensure some degree of stability for a Zimbabwe that was in a state of what could arguably be characterised as a crisis of legitimacy. Prior to the signing of the GPA, the ZANU-PF and the two MDC factions signed a Memorandum of Understanding (MoU) that outlined the issues raised by the parties that needed to be addressed for a negotiated settlement to be reached. According to Smith-Hohn (2009), issues of significance for ZANU-PF included sanctions, the land question and external interference, while the MDC was concerned about the security of its members, the prevention of violence, torture and arbitrary arrests of activists and civilians by the state, as well as the role of the SADC and African Union as underwriters and guarantors of the global political agreement that was under negotiation. The priority areas of the parties, as shown in the MoU, paint an interesting picture that gives us a glimpse into what each define as their political programme – but also of the extent to which state-sanctioned violence impacted the MDC.

Two months after the signing of the MoU, the ZANU-PF and two MDC factions finalised the GPA whose objective was to lay the foundation for the establishment of a Government of National Unity. The signing of the GPA meant that the parties would work together to restore stability in Zimbabwe. According to Mokhawa (2011), President Mugabe's decision to agree to a political agreement was the result of pressure from the international community and the SADC region, which were advising him to back down. In addition to this, the Zimbabwean economic situation was dire, and it was evident from the political pronouncements of the global community that they would not work with a ZANU-PF government that they deemed as illegitimate based on the violent elections that had cemented Mugabe's authority. Furthermore, Mokhawa adds, all Mugabe's political cards were drawn "or, as desperation discards logic as well as law, it could be argued that Mugabe was desperate" (2011:27). Tsvangirai's decision to agree to the political agreement is argued by Southall (2013 as being informed by the realisation that the MDC opting out would further complicate the political situation and the deteriorating economic conditions that were affecting Zimbabwean people.

The GPA was welcomed by international, continental, and regional bodies who saw it as a step towards the ending of political violence and economic devastation in Zimbabwe. By this time, the instability in the country had reached a crisis point, with hundreds of thousands of citizens having fled to the diaspora and the economy in freefall. The election violence had also affected relations with other SADC member states. In August 2008, the former president of Botswana, Ian Khama, refused to attend a SADC regional summit that was to take place in Johannesburg. The Botswana foreign ministry indicated that unless there is a power-sharing agreement between the ZANU-PF and MDC, the President would not avail himself for the summit (Banya, 2008). Globally, the European Union and the USA had also insisted that economic sanctions on the country would remain unless there were significant reforms put in place, including a power-sharing agreement. During the negotiation process, other SADC member states also stood up to Mugabe. In Mozambique, the regional body's organ on Politics, Defence and Security accused him of stalling the process of establishing a unity government and instructed him to respect timelines that had been established for this. It was evident that the SADC was no longer prepared to pretend that the Zimbabwean situation was not critical.

Establishing the Government of National Unity

The Government of National Unity was formed in February 2009, with the ZANU-PF's Robert Mugabe as state president, ZANU-PF's Joyce Mujuru and Joseph Msika as first and second Vice Presidents respectively, the MDC's Morgan Tsvangirai as Prime Minister, and the MDC-M's Arthur Mutambara and Thokozani Khuphe as Deputy Prime Ministers. Ministerial portfolios were shared among the parties, with the ZANU-PF having eighteen of the portfolios, the MDC thirteen and the MDC-M three. Some of the key portfolios that were assumed by the MDC included Minister of Finance and Minister of Economic Planning and Investment Promotion, while the ZANU-PF assumed the Minister of Defence and the Minister of Justice and Legal Affairs.

The allocation of portfolios was not without conflict. It exposed one of the salient challenges with the establishment of coalition governments, namely, the tensions around how to define and administer shared power. Given the country's history of political conflict as outlined, it would have been difficult for a ZANU-PF and MDC coalition to be without great difficulty from the onset. At the heart of the conflict was the Ministry of Home Affairs, which held strategic importance for both the ZANU-PF and the MDC. The Ministry of Home Affairs was likely deemed particularly important for two reasons. Firstly, one of the core functions of the Ministry is to regulate and facilitate immigration and the movement of persons through ports of entry. In a securocracy like Zimbabwe, power is derived from managing who has access to entry, which has implications for who has access to the people. Secondly, the Ministry manages the official identity and status of all persons, giving it access to data used in the development of voter registries. Identity, thus, is essential to taking part in elections. Given the country's history of disputed elections and the opposition's accusations of the ZANU-PF government's tampering with the voters' roll, it is clear why this Ministry was of particular importance to the parties. So much so, in fact, that negotiations around this portfolio led to a stalemate, resulting in the halting of the negotiation process until the following year. The political solution to the impasse was recommended by the SADC, which proposed that the Ministerial portfolio be shared on a rotating basis between the ZANU-PF and the MDC. As a result of this agreement, during the GNU, former Vice President, ZANU-PF's Kembo Mohadi and MDC's Giles Mutsekwa became co-ministers of the Home Affairs Ministry.

The GNU lasted until 2013 when Zimbabwe held harmonised elections that resulted in an overwhelming electoral victory for the ZANU-PF in both presidential and parliamentary elections. While these elections were also disputed by the opposition and deemed unfair by some institutions including Amnesty International, the violence that had been experienced in the previous elections was not repeated. Zimbabwe continues to be under ZANU-PF rule, and has not had a coalition government since then.

Outcomes of the Government of National Unity

While Zimbabwe is undoubtedly still in an exceedingly difficult political and economic state, the coalition government of 2009–2013 had significant outcomes. On the economic front, the country adopted the US dollar as a currency of exchange, which stabilised the economy after many years of hyper-inflation and the devaluing of the Zimbabwean dollar (Kumar, 2011). As a direct consequence of this, food shortages that had become chronic were alleviated as there was availability of food resources. On the political front, linked to this, was the development of a new constitution with a Bill of Rights that centred the right to vote for all Zimbabweans of voting age within the country. This constitution was unanimously endorsed by parliament. Importantly, the new constitution also made provisions for the freedom of expression and freedom of the media, which had been significantly violated over the years and particularly during the 2008 elections. According to Mokhawa (2011) and the International Crisis Group (2013), the constitutional referendum enabled the European Union to lift the restrictive measures against most of the individuals and entities it had targeted. The sanctions imposed on Zimbabwe were significantly eased.

To understand how the GNU was experienced by Zimbabwean people, it was important to engage both political players as well as ordinary people about what the country meant for them under a coalition government. In the last quarter of 2020, my research team visited Zimbabwe on a data collection mission. This was a difficult period given

23

the COVID-19 global pandemic that had resulted in a lockdown in the country, as well as strict regulations around movement and assembly. Nonetheless, the team managed to facilitate some crucial interviews and collect data. Additional data was collected from Zimbabweans in the diaspora, including some exiled former political leaders who were instrumental in the administration of the country during the period of the GNU and shortly thereafter. The three key questions the interviewees were asked were:

1. What was your experience of the GNU in the period 2009–2013?
2. How has Zimbabwe changed since the end of the GNU?
3. What is your opinion on the future realities of a coalition government in Zimbabwe?

Three political leaders from the MDC indicated that while the GNU is largely celebrated for having brought a semblance of political and economic stability in Zimbabwe, it was not an ideal arrangement and proved exceedingly difficult for the MDC due to the ZANU-PF's embeddedness in the state. According to one of the leaders who worked in the coalition government, administrators in the state had instructions from the ZANU-PF to undermine and sabotage efforts of the MDC at establishing important reforms, making it difficult for some of the agreements of the GNU to be implemented. An MDC activist based in South Africa argued that even the celebrated constitution was a serious problem because it excluded voters in the diaspora. According to him, this was aimed at usurping the growing power of the MDC that had a huge support based in the diaspora as many of those who had fled had done so to escape the authoritarian rule of the ZANU-PF regime. A student activist member of the Zimbabwe National Students Union (ZINASU) that is affiliated to the MDC concurred with this assertion. He added that even the progressive inclusions in the new constitution that centred on freedom of speech and media freedom were constantly violated as state repression did not fundamentally cease but was cleverly concealed from the watchful eyes of the world. In terms of the economy, there was general agreement that things did improve, and that the quality of life was much better under the GNU than it had been before. An MDC leader based in Harare made it clear that the only reason the economy improved was because the global community and markets function on trust, and they trusted the MDC, which importantly, was in control of the Finance Ministry.

All the MDC members interviewed stated that conditions following the end of the GNU deteriorated significantly, and that the ZANU-PF's questionable electoral victory in the 2013 harmonised elections emboldened the party. The violence in the country around 2020, which was characterised by abductions of opposition activists, including members of ZINASU, as well as the arbitrary arrests of journalists such as Hopewell Chin'ono, were cited as indications that the ruling party had no intention of respecting agreements made during the GNU. Economically, things have deteriorated since the introduction of the Real Time Gross Settlement (RTGS) dollar, a currency that is not recognised outside the borders of Zimbabwe. Despite this, none of the MDC interviewees believe that a coalition government is the answer. They contend that the ZANU-PF needs to be removed completely if Zimbabwe is to ever recover from decades of maladministration and corruption.

Four ZANU-PF leaders who were interviewed shared sentiments similar to their MDC counterparts, arguing that power-sharing would not be sustainable. However, unlike MDC activists, their experience of the GNU is more positive, with all of them stating that the coalition government alleviated the violence that had come to define the Zimbabwean political milieu. Of significance to them was that the international community was less harsh on the coalition government, enabling the country to recover a little of its international reputation. One interviewee who served in the coalition government indicated that the international community's softening attitude towards the Zimbabwean government could even be experienced in international trips where the country's delegation was treated with a degree of regard that it had not been afforded previously. The trust in the government also saw an increase in remittances from the diaspora, according to the gentleman.

Nine people spread across five of the ten provinces were interviewed. Their composition was as follows: three from Harare (Harare Province), one from Chivhu (Mashonaland East Province), two from Masvingo (Masvingo Province), two from Bulawayo (Bulawayo Province) and one from Kadoma (Mashonaland West Province). These individuals indicated that the GNU was the most economically and politically stable the country had been since 2000. They stated that service delivery was better under the GNU, and that they trusted the coalition government because of the MDC being present in it and having important portfolios such as Finance and Health. The interviewees from Harare Province lauded food security as the most important outcome of the GNU, while the interviewees from both Mashonaland Provinces cited diminished political violence as the most significant outcome. The most positive of the interviewees were from Bulawayo, who argued that for them, the issue was not only political or economic, but also that they felt that their concerns were taken seriously by the government under the GNU. All this, the interviewees apart from one from Masvingo stated, has changed since the end of the GNU as things have returned to what they were in terms of economic difficulty and police brutality. One of the participants from Masvingo indicated that things have remained relatively the same for her as Masvingo had always been relatively better than other parts of the country in terms of service delivery. In Bulawayo, it appears that service delivery has deteriorated to a point of being deemed a violation of human rights. The participants indicated that even the most fundamental resource, water, became very scarce after the GNU and has now become completely unavailable.

For these people and others who were interviewed in South Africa and the broader diaspora, the future of Zimbabwe lies in the removal of ZANU-PF from power. However, many of them indicated that in the absence of that, they would much rather return to the GNU. A medical doctor practising outside of Zimbabwe, who left the country in 2015, stated that during the GNU he was able to save a lot of money that he had hoped to invest, but that soon after the 2013 harmonised elections, he had lost everything after the economy tanked once again. In his opinion, a single-party government in Zimbabwe is disastrous for the country's economy since the international community has no faith in the ZANU-PF regime and thus would not invest in or even avail aid to the country.

Analysis of the Primary Data

Based on the data collected as well as a study of available research, there is evidence that the GNU was an important and welcome intervention in Zimbabwe, and that it managed to bring about economic and political stability. This is congruent with arguments that have been posed by scholars such as Kadima and Lembani (2006) who argue that coalition governments can foster cohesion. And while Kadima's work focuses largely on the coalition government in Mauritius, his analysis can be transposed to Zimbabwe based on its own history of conflict and national disunity resulting from systematic tribalism and the politics of ethnic rivalry that were somewhat alleviated in Mauritius by the formation of an ethnically and regionally representative coalition government. In the case of Zimbabwe, however, the coalition government was mainly aimed at resolving the immediate political problems rather than deeper issues that contribute to the nation's disunity – and this might be one of the GNU's failures that need to be reflected on. Earlier in this chapter, I touched on Gukurahundi with the deliberate intention of situating it in the broader conversation around Zimbabwe's contemporary political crisis. It is not possible to make sense of the problems in Zimbabwe today without understanding how the violence of the 1980s set parameters for the violence that defines the country today, and importantly, the tribal and ethnic tensions whose persistence undermines the capacity for the country to achieve genuine unity. The coalition government in Mauritius intentionally placed the issue of tribal and ethnic unity at its centre – something which should have been done in Zimbabwe to address some of the deeper underlying issues that inform the tensions between the state and sections of the populace.

The end of the GNU has seen Zimbabwe descend into the chaotic state that characterised it prior to its signing of the Global Political Agreement. In 2020, while the world was experiencing a crisis in the form of the COVID-19 global pandemic, Zimbabwe was battling a different pandemic: the re-emergence of political violence and the arbitrary arrest of journalists and opposition activists. The violation of human rights by Zimbabwean security forces resulted in loud calls by the international community for the country to be held accountable for the actions of its government, which included the opening of live ammunition on protesters and systematic abductions of student activists. In South Africa, opposition parties called on the Zimbabwean Embassy to be shut down. In August 2020, a group of Zimbabwean citizens and South Africans marched in solidarity to the

Zimbabwean Embassy in Tshwane, protesting the arrests and abductions. Soon there-after, in what was reminiscent of the pre-GPA scenario, President Cyril Ramaphosa, who at the time was serving as the Chair of the SADC, announced that former Government Minister, Sydney Mufamadi, and former National Assembly Speaker, Baleka Mbete, had been appointed as special envoys to Zimbabwe to identify ways South Africa can assist the country to overcome its problems.

Evidently, the GNU, while it was certainly an important development, provided tempo-rary relief for the deeply embedded structural problems that Zimbabwe is confronted with. It is an important point to reflect on that while all participants are of the view that life in Zimbabwe was better under the GNU, there are conflicting views about the future realities of coalition governments in the country, grounded in the opinion that it would be much better under a single-party government, with most participants saying the government should be of the MDC-Alliance. This perspective offers us important insight into the strengths and pitfalls of coalition governments and how they are expe-rienced. That there were significant changes in the Zimbabwean economy and the lives of ordinary people is evident in their responses as well as the existing data and litera-ture on the state of socio-economic and political conditions in Zimbabwe in the period 2009-2013. This, however, is not enough, at least for most of the people interviewed for this book, to negate the growing opinion that the ZANU-PF regime is unsustainable and thus requires annihilation.

While the sample size for the exploration of the Zimbabwean question in the context of coalition governments is not adequate to make an absolute proclamation on the general feelings of ordinary Zimbabweans about the future of coalition governments, what little was gleaned by my research team and I is that there is no appetite in Zimbabwe for a coalition government, largely because the historical deeds and failures of the ZANU-PF government are insurmountable and likely, irredeemable. For this reason, any party that enters such an arrangement with the ZANU-PF is regarded as a temporary buffer to the structural and institutionalised problems of the country rather than as an instrument that will facilitate meaningful and permanent change. Additionally, there is a sense that the Zimbabwean state can only really function if the MDC-Alliance is afforded space to govern on its own rather than in a Government of National Unity (GNU) or any form of coalition government. This is informed greatly by the experiences of government practitioners who were part of the GNU in both the executive and administration, who felt that the entrenchment of the ZANU-PF in the state posed many great impediments to the implementation of innovative programmes that were introduced or championed by MDC officials.

Another important observation as pertains to Zimbabwe is that we see, once again, the relevance and future of former national liberation movements cum governing parties questioned. The ZANU-PF's legitimacy as a governing party has been obliterated by decades of misrule and we have seen in the recent past the tendency to resort to militarisation as a mechanism for maintaining a hold on power. This, unfortunately, is the trend across the continent and examples are abundant of former national liberation movements morphing into instruments of suppression who rule with a margin of terror. As the youth of South Africa posited towards the 2016 local government elections, we must reflect on why the challenges of today demand not a struggle history but a new imagination of how to fashion a higher civilisation and entertain the idea of politics that are young in posture, orientation, and representation.

3

THE COALITION EXPERIENCE IN SOUTH AFRICAN LOCAL, DISTRICT AND METROPOLITAN MUNICIPALITIES: 2016 – 2021

The Economy in 2016

The 2016 local government elections – the fifth held in South Africa since the dawn of democracy – were held on 3 August. Millions of eligible South Africans cast their votes to elect local, district and metropolitan municipalities across all nine provinces. The economic climate leading up to these elections was dire. The country's economy had contracted by 0.3 percent quarter-on-quarter (seasonally adjusted and annualised), plunging economic growth into negative territory. The mining and manufacturing sectors were experiencing significant decline – with the former contracting by 11.5 percent owing to a decline in the production of coal, gold and other metal ores including platinum and iron ore (Statistics SA, 2016). Manufacturing saw a contraction of over three percent owing primarily to slow production in manufacturing sectors related to food and beverages, petroleum and chemicals, and transport equipment (Statistics SA, 2016). And while the unadjusted real GDP increased by 0.7 percent year-on-year in the fourth quarter of 2016, and all provinces – apart from Mpumalanga Province and the Free State Province – had recorded positive economic growth rates in comparison to previous years, this was not enough to offset the devastation that had been wrought by the declining contributions to the economy by the primary and secondary sectors (Statistics SA, 2016). The implications of this were growing levels of unemployment and poverty, and the widening inequality gap that saw the poor become poorer and the rich become richer.

Unemployment levels in 2016 hit a 12-year high. The country's unemployment rate stood at 26.7 percent in the first quarter of 2016. The expanded unemployment rate, which includes people who stopped looking for work, stood at 36.3 percent. The results of the Quarterly Labour Force Survey for the fourth quarter of 2016 released by Statistics South Africa indicated that employment grew by 235 000 and the number of job seekers declined by 92 000. Among the hardest hit sectors were construction and manufacturing, which saw quarterly employment drops of 88 000 and 80 000, respectively.

Other critical industries also saw significant job losses – leading to one of the worst job bloodbaths the country had ever seen. The youth aged 15-34 years were the most group vulnerable in the labour market. The youth unemployment rate stood at a debilitating 37.1 percent – which was 10.6 percentage points above the national average (Statistics SA, 2016). Importantly, the race factor in unemployment was especially pronounced in this period. Over the period 2008 to 2016, the incidence of long-term unemployment was highest among Black Africans with as many as 61.0 to 71.0 percent of that group looking for work for one year or longer. The unemployment rate among the White population group – ranging between 4.1 percent in 2008 and 7.3 percent in 2014 – was the lowest of all the population groups by a large margin. In 2014, Black Africans accounted for 79.3 percent of the working age population, but they were under-represented among the employed and over-represented among the unemployed, at 85.7 percent, and the not economically active population at 83.3 percent (Statistics SA, 2016). The situation was identical in 2016 and continues on a similar trajectory today.

By the time the 2016 local government elections took place, many Black people had been hurled into a zone of economic inactivity and marginalisation. We had entered the third decade of democracy and while change was happening, to many, it was at a glacial pace. Millions of Black people were increasingly feeling alienated from the South Africa that the governing party had characterised as a country alive with possibilities, and this alienation gave way to a feeling of collective rage and dejection.

The Rise in Crime

The socio-economic climate was also impacted significantly by these economic realities. With growing levels of unemployment, the country also saw a marked increase in crime. According to the crime report released by the South African Police Service (SAPS) for the year 2016, nearly all categories of crime were on an upward trajectory. The murder rate increased marginally from 34 to 34.1 per 100 000 people, with an average of 52.1 people murdered each day. Sexual assaults, robbery with aggravating circumstances, house robberies and hijacking of cars also saw a marked increase. Other crimes that saw an increase include drug-related offenses which include use, possession of and dealing in drugs. In the 2016/17 period of reporting, the police recorded 292 689 drug-related offenses, translating to an average of 801.9 offences each day. This means that 524.1 drug-related crimes were recorded for every 100 000 people in the country. And while crimes such as rape and common assault saw a decline, with the assault rate decreasing from 301.1 to 280.2 per 100 000 people and rape decreasing from 75.7 to 71.3 per 100 000, various researchers including the Institute for Security Studies (2016) made the valid point that the decreases could not be taken as an accurate measure of either the extent or trend of the crimes. This is due in part to the notorious under-reporting rate for rape in South Africa resulting from low prosecution and conviction rates for perpetrators, and the chronic distrust of the criminal justice system by ordinary people, among other factors. The unreliability of common assault statistics stems from the fact that most victims do not report these crimes to the police since the victim and perpetrator may be related, such as in a case of domestic violence. Victims are thus often reluctant to report assault.

What is evident from the crime statistics in this period is that economic crimes were on the increase. These are crimes that are committed by individuals or groups specifically for economic gain. The correlation between inequality and crime has been found in empirical literature. The Development Policy Research Unit at the University of Cape Town released a report in 2017 titled *The socio-economic determinants of crime in South Africa: An empirical assessment*, which combined published crime statistics with demographic data from the 2011 South African Census Community Profiles to investigate which socio-economic factors attract crime at a police precinct level. The research determined that resource-acquisition driven crimes such as robberies are attracted by high levels of income and inequality and low levels of unemployment. The research also found a positive relationship between violent crime and income: that at high levels of precinct-level income, violent crime decreased. These results are universal. Dr Kostadis J. Papaioannou, a Postdoctoral Research Associate at the Department of International Development at the London School of Economics and Political Science, in a paper titled "Hunger makes a thief of any man: Poverty and crime in British colonial Asia" uses rainfall variation as an instrumental variable for rice production to estimate the impact of poverty on different types of crime across British colonies in South and South East Asia. Using original primary sources retrieved from annual administrative and statistical reports, it provides some of the first evidence in a historical setting on the causal relationship between poverty and crime. Papaioannou demonstrates how extreme rainfall, both droughts and floods, led to a large increase in property crimes including robberies in colonial Asia. Dong, Egger and Guo (2020) make a similar analysis about the crime in China. In their paper titled "Is poverty the mother of crime? Evidence from homicide rates in China", they contend that poverty and low-income level is positively related to homicide rates. They demonstrate how the internal rural-urban migration from more poor and violent localities contributes to the destination cities' homicide rates. The poverty-homicide association implies that absolute deprivation is mainly responsible for violent crime.

If the argument by Marcus Aurelius that "poverty is the mother of crime" is true, then it is evident that the 2016 local government elections that took place in an environment of economic difficulty were inevitably going to occur in a high crime environment. And while no crime is victimless, economic crimes are especially devastating to individuals, families and communities. They view these crimes as a failure by the government to institute law and order, thereby protecting the citizenry. It is thus not surprising that in environments of high crime, there is serious conflict and distrust by citizens towards the police and the criminal justice system, translating into distrust and anger towards the government.

Popular Protests and Youth Participation

In 2016 there were also great socio-political tensions in various spheres of South African life. Of significance were the nation-wide protests in institutions of higher learning, under the banner of the #FeesMustFall movement. Parameters for the establishment of the movement had been set the year prior by the #RhodesMustFall movement that had started at the University of Cape Town (UCT) in March 2015. The movement was aimed at highlighting issues of coloniality in historically White institutions across South Africa and used statues and monuments of colonialism and apartheid as symbols of the said struggle. The most notable act of protest by the #RhodesMustFall movement occurred on 9 March when a small group of student activists at UCT desecrated the statue of British mining magnate imperialist Cecil John Rhodes. The students threw faeces at the statue, arguing that it was a symbol of an amoral past that continues to haunt and define the lives of the oppressed Black majority in South Africa. This incident would give rise to open dialogue at the university and various others across the country about the necessity for the decolonisation of higher education. Just seven months later, the #FeesMustFall movement would be born and with it, unprecedented mobilisation and organising by students across the political divide.

The #FeesMustFall movement brought inequalities in South African higher education into sharp focus. Although higher education had always been a site of struggle, with many protests having been staged in various institutions since time immemorial, the significance of the #FeesMustFall movement was that every higher learning institu-tion was involved. In the past, historically Black institutions in particular had waged struggles against the exorbitant cost of education, but this had not garnered as much attention from the public or the media. It wasn't until all universities were rendered ungovernable by protesting students that the issue was elevated to national discourse. While #FeesMustFall initially began as a struggle against the fee increment that had been proposed by the then Department of Higher Education and Training (DHET), it soon included many other broader issues including the institutionalised racism, the lingering colonial edifice in higher education, the outsourcing of workers in universities and spatial injustice (Mahlatsi, 2018). The latter issue would see the movement forge alliances with community-based organisations and non-government organisations that were fighting against unemployment and related issues within communities. The #FeesMustFall movement thus became a mobilising force for popular struggles beyond the confines of higher education. It thrust to the forefront the systematic challenges confronting working-class youth and Black communities. The period leading up to the 2016 local government elections was marked by heightened youth politicisation that went beyond the confines of university halls. Communities across the country also saw increased levels of youth participation in service delivery protests. These protests were not only becoming more frequent but were increasingly becoming more militant in their posture and orientation.

Of significance about the #FeesMustFall movement is that most higher learning institutions in South Africa are in urban areas. It is undebatable that this had an impact on the electoral outcomes of the 2016 local government elections. The governing African National Congress saw an unprecedented decline in voter support in urban areas. Importantly, the number of youth voters across the country increased slightly from the previous local government elections in 2011. In those elections, a total of 23 654 347 people registered to vote and a total number of 13 592 856 votes were cast – reflecting 57.5 percent of registered voters. Of the registered voters, 8.3 million were youth, with 4.2 million of them turning out to vote (Independent Electoral Commission, 2011). This translates to only 50.6 percent of youth casting their votes. The situation was slightly different in 2016, where 6.3 million youth cast their votes, translating to roughly 53 percent of youth votes (Independent Electoral Commission, 2017). Evidently, youth voter turn-out in South Africa is patently low. Various studies have examined youth participation in the country, making various credible arguments to explain youth voter apathy. A comprehensive report by the Mapungubwe Institute for Strategic Reflection (MISTRA) titled *Voting trends 25 years into democracy: Analysis of South Africa's 2019 election* contains a full section focusing specifically on youth participation. The analysis tracks national and municipal registration, and turnout trends, among South African youth since 1999. It argues that the boycotting of elections by the youth is a historical trend, and that this is the result of alienation from electoral politics. Quoting Imran Buccus (2019), the report contends:

> *Such alienation should be viewed in the context of the day-to-day realities of this grouping because they are the ones that suffer the most when it comes to limited access to socio-economic opportunities. These age groups are the ones who face very high unemployment, for instance. Thus, the alienation occurs among those who have benefitted least in society from economic inclusion. This may have dangerous implications for South Africa's still young democracy...*

This situation with low youth voter turnout has cemented the simplistic narrative that seeks to suggest that young people are apathetic and uninterested in politics. Empirical evidence suggests that this is not a true reflection of the feelings of young people. Over the years, various think-tanks, including the Institute for Security Studies (2016), have conducted qualitative research aimed at better understanding the factors that inform the voting patterns and political activism of South African youth. Shortly before the 2016 local government elections, the institute released a report titled "Do you want my vote? Understanding the factors that influence voting among young South Africans". The monograph, through responses and comments made by thousands of South African students aged 18 to 24 years in rural and urban areas across all nine provinces, provided a detailed picture of young people's perceptions of politics and of the factors that influence their participation in elections. One of the key findings of this study was that young people were neither apathetic nor were they ignorant of the political dynamics in the country. While they held strong views on the political realities of the country, and their location within them, they felt alienated from formal politics, as the MISTRA report would corroborate three years later. They had intense distrust for politicians and political parties. In addition to this, and of great significance, the study found that many of them had negative experiences of government agencies and departments from which they required services. It was the general feeling of young people that their concerns were deliberately ignored by political leaders and that they were constantly being thrust into situations where they needed to resort to violence to be heard. This argument was also raised by university students during the #FeesMustFall protests.

Another important argument that was finding expression in the youth during this period was that the pace of transformation in post-apartheid South Africa was painfully slow. Many young people argued that while they were constantly being referred to as the "Mandela generation" that had the gift of democracy bestowed upon them, they were experiencing systematic challenges that were born of apartheid. This sentiment had been expressed two years before the election by social activist and lead researcher of this book, Malaika Mahlatsi (Wa Azania) who in her 2014 bestselling book, *Memoirs of a Born Free: Reflections on the Rainbow Nation*, had argued that the edifice of apartheid was continuing to define the lives of the so-called "born free" generation that had inherited poverty and inequalities from their parents. The Institute for Security Studies (2016) report also indicated that young people were arguing that they had witnessed elections before, and that their parents and older family members had voted. Despite this, meaningful change was yet to happen in their communities where the scourge of unemployment and poverty was persistent. Of significance about these reflections is that the ANC as the governing party stood as a symbol of the slow pace of transformation in the eyes of the youth. In this climate, where the youth felt alienated and were growing increasingly frustrated with political parties and the institution of government, it was inevitable that they would not cast their votes. It was also clear from the political climate at the time that many of those who had a desire to cast their votes were looking for an alternative – a party that they felt best represented their aspirations in a way that the ANC was not seen to be doing.

It is not an accident of history that at the time when young voters were feeling alienated from the governing party, the Economic Freedom Fighters (EFF) emerged as the credible alternative for them. The organisation was raising issues of great significance to the youth voter – issues that had in fact been initiated by the ANC in previous national conferences, but which had not been attended to. As far back as the 52nd National Conference that took place in Polokwane in 2007, the ANC had already taken the resolution to progressively introduce free education for the poor until undergraduate level. By the time students took to the streets in protest, the resolution was almost a decade old. That the EFF used the issue of free education as its electoral commitment was reflective of the ANC's own lack of political will to resolve the matter. Nature abhors a vacuum, and when the ANC created the space, it alienated young voters who, in response, sought an alternative in the opposition. This increasing dejection by the youth towards the ANC was a blunder for which the party paid dearly.

A Fractured ANC

Reflections on the socio-economic and political climate leading up to the 2016 local government elections would be an exercise in historical revisionism if they do not touch on the state of the ANC at that time. While it is true that the above-mentioned factors played a significant role in shaping the election outcomes, the state of the organisation also had a colossal role to play. In fact, some might even argue that the internal challenges that the ANC was confronted with leading up to these elections made other external factors insurmountable. And yet, my own assessment is that the challenges that the organisation was faced with were deeply historical and had been germinating long before they erupted in the spectacular fashion in which they did. It is not the purpose of this book to delve into the history of the ANC and the systemic fractures that the organisation has experienced over time. As such, some of the challenges alluded to will be analysed briefly, solely for the purpose of contextualising the posture and orientation of the organisation at the said time and space.

The period leading up to the 2016 local government elections was a nightmare for the ANC-led government in terms of public image. The organisation was faced with crises of governance, with numerous state-owned enterprises teetering on the brink of collapse; government deployees being embroiled in issues of corruption, maladministration, and misappropriation of state funds across various departments and state agencies; and perhaps more significantly, the perennial attacks on the person of the then president and his office. The Nkandla imbroglio, often referred to in the media as "Nkandlagate", was at the centre of this image crisis and would create immeasurable problems for the organisation's election campaign. Nkandla, the private home of the then president, Jacob Gedleyihlekisa Zuma, was at the centre of controversy following the release of a report by the former Public Protector, Advocate Thuli Madonsela, which found that the president had unduly benefitted from improvements made to his home. Public funds had been used to make improvements to the home, and while most of them were for security reasons, it was later determined that some were merely aesthetic. The project had cost taxpayers over R246 million (Makatile, 2016) and it became a huge controversy given the state of the economy as explained. The matter was subjected to the courts by the two biggest opposition parties, the DA and the EFF, and would ultimately find its way to the Constitutional Court, which ruled that the president and the ANC-majority national assembly had failed to uphold the country's Constitution after failing to comply with the Public Protector's report recommendations, which recommended, among other things, that a portion of the money used for the upgrades be paid back to the National Treasury. Subsequent to the Constitutional Court ruling, the former president paid back nearly R8 million as directed by the Public Protector's report. Hoever, by this time, significant damage had been done to the ANC brand, which was characterised by many as corrupt and incapable of self-correction.

The damage was not only to the ANC's image but also to the organisation internally. The Nkandla imbroglio created a climate of heightened divisions within the party and the broader Mass Democratic Movement (MDM), with some members of the organisation and liberation struggle stalwarts openly calling for the resignation of President Zuma. Rivonia trialists, the late Isithwalandwe Ahmed Kathrada and former chairperson of the party's Integrity Committee, the late Isithwalandwe Andrew Mlangeni, were among those who publicly condemned the then sitting president and demanded his voluntary departure from office. Some ANC leaders and branches of the organisation also made similar calls. Some ANC regional leaders interviewed for this book alluded to the fact that they were deeply uncomfortable using the image of President Zuma in their campaigns due to the difficulties around his name at the time. This was despite the long-standing tradition in the ANC that the party's president would be the face of its election campaign. Similar sentiments had been expressed going towards the 2014 general elections, with the chairperson of the ANC in the Gauteng Province, David Makhura, having stated that the former president, Thabo Mbeki, would be used to appeal to the Black middle-class voter who did not identify with the then sitting president, Jacob Zuma (*City Press*, 2013). The insinuation was pellucid: the image of President Zuma, symbolically and literally, was unpalatable to particular voters. This narrative cemented the idea that an ANC leader could be isolated from the organisation – and that this was correct. A few years later, following the 2016 local government elections, the ANC National Executive Committee (NEC) would state that it took collective responsibility for the results, much to the chagrin of many members and voters, who had been socialised into the deeply problematic idea that the organisation should isolate its leader.

There were also significant challenges at local level, where the ANC witnessed unprec-edented protests over candidates' lists for municipal councils. The protests were widespread, affecting most of the provinces in the country. In the KwaZulu-Natal Province, the Congress Movement was torn asunder by these protests. The Communist Party's Durban Region had threatened to abandon the ANC's campaign over claims that fraudulent candidates were being imposed on ANC branches. Towards the elections, ten members of the ANC had indicated that they would stand as independent candidates due to the alleged side-lining of supporters of the then former ANC Provincial Chairperson, Senzo Mchunu. Mchunu had resigned as Premier of the province following a failed bid for second term as the organisation's chairperson. So intense were the challenges in KwaZulu-Natal that members of the organisation took to the streets to protest. Similar action was taken in Gauteng where members of the organisation staged protests out-side the ANC Head Office, Luthuli House, arguing that their grievances in relation to the alleged fraudulent lists from Ekurhuleni and Tshwane regions were ignored.

In the Eastern Cape Province, members of the organisation blocked buses from leaving party headquarters in Port Elizabeth where candidates were on their way to be vetted before their names could be submitted to the Independent Electoral Commission (IEC).

As was the case in KwaZulu-Natal and Gauteng provinces, the members were arguing that their preferred candidates had been deliberately side-lined and not included in the list for municipal councillors. Additionally, several ANC councillors also took the decision to stand as independent candidates. ANC members stood as independent candidates in some of the most strategic wards in the Nelson Mandela Bay Metropolitan Municipality, which the ANC would ultimately lose to a Democratic Alliance-led coalition. The Western Cape Province, which had long been lost to the DA, was not spared the conflicts. In what was an unprecedented move, the ANC in the province had to postpone the launch of its election manifesto due to the in-fighting. Members of the organisation had been engaged in protests outside the party's provincial headquarters in Cape Town, arguing that the list process had not been democratic and that some names were illegally imposed. Police had to be involved in this conflict when the Deputy Provincial Secretary and a senior staff member were locked in their offices and prevented from leaving by protesting members.

The North-West Province was without doubt one of the most troubled provinces leading up to the elections. On various occasions, ANC members stormed Gertrude Mphekwa House, the party's provincial headquarters in Mahikeng, crying foul over the list process. Three former ANC mayors, of Moretele, Taung and Madibeng, joined the DA on the eve of elections. Ten ANC councillors registered to contest elections under a newly established organisation, Forum 4 Service Delivery, dealing a blow to the organisation at a time when it was haemorrhaging electoral support. Another significant blow to the ANC and the broader mass democratic movement happened in the Free State Province where the SACP contested the elections against the ANC in the highly contested Metsimaholo Local Municipality. While the ANC would maintain plurality in the municipality, it would subsequently lose power to a DA, EFF and the Metsimaholo Community Association (MCA) coalition.

These fractures impacted how leaders and ordinary members of the organisation related to one another. Significantly, they had implications for electoral campaigning, which depends greatly on organisational unity and the communication of a single message. That a house divided from within cannot stand has been proven throughout history and it was no exception in this instance. The ANC went into the 2016 local government elections as a divided and battered organisation and the election results were the evidence. Subsequent by-elections across the country would demonstrate what we know to be true: that a united ANC is able to win elections convincingly. But what is clear is that the 2016 local government elections took place under exceedingly difficult circumstances economically, socio-politically, and otherwise. The analysis of the interviews with government practitioners who were instrumental in the formation of coalitions across various metropolitan municipalities will expand on some of the internal challenges that confronted the ANC that also had an impact on the outcome of the said elections.

An Implosion that the Organisation and Experts Saw Coming

While some members of the ANC were stunned by the results of the 2016 local government elections, where the governing party lost three metros to opposition coalition governments (an exception is made of the City of Ekurhuleni where the ANC leads the coalition), some within the organisation already knew that the elections would be extremely difficult. Two ANC leaders in the City of Johannesburg and the City of Tshwane who were interviewed for this book indicated that their own internal analysis of the prevailing balance of forces gave an indication that the party was in serious trouble at least a year before the elections. They both argued that branches within the metros had been so severely divided by internal fighting that it was impossible for the ANC to campaign effectively. As one of them said: "Even without the other global and local factors that defined the political moment towards the elections, it would have been extremely difficult if not altogether impossible for the ANC to win. The alliance was more divided than it had ever been in the democratic dispensation and there was no appetite on the part of the ANC leadership to meaningfully engage its alliance partners to steer the ship back on course". In the City of Tshwane, the interviewee argued, the tensions were so devastating that even Regional Executive Committee meetings were reduced to spectres of a political cold war that had gripped the metro. The climate, he argued, was one of war rather than campaigning for an ANC victory.

But it was not only internal political fractures that were undermining the organisation's chance at electoral victory. According to an ANC regional leader in the Nelson Mandela Bay Metro, the organisation was also faced with a resource crisis so that there was not enough money to run the election campaign. This argument was corroborated by former senior state official and ANC leader Crispian Olver, who had been sent to Nelson Mandela Bay Metro just over a year before the elections to root out corruption in the municipality. According to Olver, by April 2016, just four months before the elections, the party's fundraising account was virtually empty after money donated to the organisation was effectively looted by two known ANC Youth League regional leaders. Olver, in *How to steal a city: The battle for Nelson Mandela Bay*, states: "I came from my fundraising experience feeling grubby and sordid. On top of everything, it had been ineffective: by May 2016, with only two months to go before the local election, we were heading for a severe cash crunch. How was the ANC going to finance its campaign?" (Olver, 2017:149). Another regional leader in the Bay also indicated that while the coffers of the organisation were running dry, individual leaders were well-resourced from proceeds of unethical and possibly criminal activities that had further soiled the name of the ANC in the metro. The conduct of ANC leaders working in the municipality, he contended, was solely responsible for the election outcomes in the Bay Metro, for they had completely eroded the public's trust in the organisation. According to him, it was obvious that the party would not win the election, and it was often discussed in private even as publicly, a sense of optimism was being displayed. Asked why these concerns were raised privately but not with the national leadership of the organisation, he responded: "They knew exactly what was happening. They knew we were on the verge of losing the metro".

Furthermore, experts had already predicted that the ANC would lose the country's big metros. Months before the elections, the Centre for Politics and Research stated that the party would lose the City of Johannesburg, the City of Tshwane, and Nelson Mandela Metro Bay (Vorster, 2016). But even before this, in 2015, Moody's Investors Service had warned that the ANC would lose the country's big cities in the following year's elections. At the time, the ratings agency had just changed the country's rating outlook from stable to negative, arguing that there was a rising risk of fiscal slippages in the face of slower growth and increasing political pressures; and increased probability that growth would remain low for a prolonged period due to structural challenges facing the mining industry and other critical sectors of the economy. The ratings agency added: "Moody's notes that while the South African government is not known for ramping up spending ahead of elections because of its disciplined fiscal framework, the potential for losses of several important cities represents a deeper challenge than the ANC has faced since the democratic transition in 1994" (*BusinessTech*, 2015).

Evidently, while the election results were devastating, there had been an indication at least a year prior to the outcome that the ANC could lose the country's key metros. Whether this was taken very seriously is perhaps a reflection for the ANC itself.

The Interview Processes

Primary data collection took the form of interviews, which were made especially difficult by the National State of Disaster regulations imposed in response to the COVID-19 global pandemic. Between 2020 and 2021, several political players and administrators across the country were interviewed for this book. Some of the interviews, such as those in the City of Ekurhuleni, the City of Tshwane, and some parts of the Free State Province, were conducted face-to-face due in part to some sensitivities with information sharing. But most of the interviews were conducted virtually as inter-provincial movement was often not possible. All interviews were recorded to ensure correct capturing of the ideas and arguments posed by the interviewees. While the lead researcher was responsible for capturing the information, I was present at all interviews to probe for information that would not have been readily shared.

The interviews were semi-structured. This kind of interview is a qualitative data collection strategy in which the researcher asks informants a series of predetermined but open-ended questions. Since a semi-structured interview is a combination of an unstructured interview and a structured interview, it has the advantages of both. The interviewees can express their opinions and ask questions of the interviewer during the interview, which encourages them to give more useful information, such as their opinions toward sensitive issues, to the qualitative research. And they could more easily give the reasons for their answers during the interviews. Additionally, the structured part of semi-structured interviews gives the interviewers reliable, comparable qualitative data. This results in the production of rich data, including observational data.

The master-themes that emerged were guided by the following questions:

1. What was the political climate that resulted in the advent of a coalition government in this metro?

    -   Broadly, the socio-economic environment that informed voter apathy or change of historical voting patterns.
    -   The intra-party dynamics that resulted in organisational fractures (if any).

2. How was the coalition constituted?

    -   An exploration of the process of negotiation and engagement with coalition partners.
    -   The salient challenges that arose in the negotiation and engagement process and how these were resolved (if at all).
    -   The ideological considerations that informed the coalition.

3. What has been the experience of governing through a coalition?

    -   The specific challenges and trials that have emerged in the term.
    -   The opportunities that a coalition government has presented in terms of service delivery.
    -   What, if any, have been legislative hurdles that presented themselves in the coalition?

4. What are the lessons learned?

    -   What needs to be done differently to ensure better coalition governance in the future?

5. Are coalitions an inevitable future for South Africa? Why or why not?

Although these questions were aimed specifically at government practitioners and political players who were directly involved in the constitution of coalition governments, the last question was posed to political leaders of local, district and metropolitan municipalities that are not in coalitions. There are several reasons for this, but at the heart of it is that to understand the future of coalition governments in South Africa, it is important to gauge the current thinking of all political players. While those in coalitions could share their experiences, those who are not in coalitions could provide insight into how coalitions ought to be constituted, and whether they have a place in the civilisation that is under perennial construction. Some few interviews were conducted with ordinary people, specifically to understand how they experienced coalition governments. As with the Zimbabwean case study, it is always important to factor in the experiences of voters because while they exist outside the political battles in Councils, they are impacted by the decisions taken in these Councils. In the City of Tshwane, for example, the political wrangling that resulted in the metro being placed under administration had devastating consequences for citizens as service delivery was affected.

Coalition Governments in South Africa: 2016-2021

Results of the interviews will be detailed per local, district and metropolitan municipality. The three metros of focus are the City of Tshwane, the City of Johannesburg, and Nelson Mandela Bay Municipality because they are the metros won by an opposition coalition. While the City of Ekurhuleni is also governed through a coalition, it is important to note that this is an ANC-led coalition as the party obtained most of the votes there. Metsimaholo Local Municipality is also analysed. While it is not a metropolitan municipality, important dynamics played themselves out in Metsimaholo, including the divisions within the Congress Movement that are at the heart of the ANC's haemorrhaging of electoral support. Additionally, Metsimaholo Local Municipality, as a historical ANC stronghold, offers us an important glimpse into how and why South Africans are increasingly becoming dejected with the organisation. It also demonstrates how power is lost in pockets – an important point that is central to the argument in this book, about the qualitative and quantitative weakening of the ANC and broader Mass Democratic Movement.

City of Johannesburg

The loss of power in the City of Johannesburg, the country's economic hub, was without doubt one of the most devastating outcomes of the 2016 local government elections for the ANC. While the party won 44.5 percent of the vote, it was unable to claim outright victory as this did not constitute the majority vote. The main opposition party, the DA, won 38.4 percent of the vote, also far short of a majority. It was the EFF, with 11 percent of the vote, that would ultimately become the kingmaker in Johannesburg. The party had made it clear from the outset that it would not enter into a coalition with the ANC, and so it came as no surprise that it entered into one with the DA. The ANC, for the first time since the dawn of democracy, found itself sitting in opposition benches in a city that had once been one of its urban strongholds.

The first Council meeting of the DA-led coalition in the City of Johannesburg was an indication of what was to come – although at the time no one knew how fractured the coalition government would become, or that the ANC would ultimately somewhat reclaim its footing within the Council. On 22 August 2016, the City held its first Council meeting to elect a Mayor. The meeting lasted an astonishing 11 hours and was punctuated by conflict between opposition party members and the Independent Electoral Commission, which had the unenviable task of fielding endless objections and managing heated tensions. Tragically, an ANC councillor who had just been sworn in earlier, Cllr Nonhlanhla Mthembu, collapsed and later died at the City Hall where the Council meeting was being held. These ominous occurrences at the City's inaugural Council meeting set parameters for future meetings that would also be characterised by instability. Cllrs Herman Mashaba and Vasco da Gama of the DA were elected as the Mayor and Speaker of Council, respectively. Neither of them would finish his term in office.

To make sense of the collapse of the DA-led coalition in government, it is important to understand the man who was at its centre – Herman Mashaba. Mashaba, prior to entering politics, was one of the most influential businesspeople in the country. His influence was derived from being the founder of hair product company, Black Like Me, which became the biggest hair brand in South Africa. Mashaba achieved this feat at the height of apartheid. Black Like Me was launched in 1985 – the year in which the apartheid government under PW Botha declared a State of Emergency following an upsurge in violent resistance to the apartheid regime. According to his autobiography, *Black Like You: Herman Mashaba, an autobiography*, he had to fight extremely hard against the dehumanising laws of apartheid and the systems put in place to make it impossible for a Black-owned business to gain access to markets and succeed. Mashaba's company continued to grow in the new dispensation, making him one of the most successful and richest Black entrepreneurs. Between 2012 and 2014, he served as the chairperson of the Free Market Foundation, a libertarian think tank deeply committed to unfettered capitalism. But as a self-proclaimed capitalist, it was fitting that Mashaba would chair an institution that believes in market fundamentalism. Equally fitting was that when he joined politics in 2015, it was as a member of the liberal Democratic Alliance whose own politics are very intricately linked to those of the Free Market Foundation that he had chaired. It was in December of that year, just eight months before the 2016 local government elections, that Mashaba announced that he would accept the nomination to stand as the DA mayoral candidate for the City of Johannesburg.

Part of Mashaba's appeal to the electorate was his stance on issues that are polarising in society, particularly on the questions of migration and crime. Throughout his campaign, Mashaba had vocalised his support for the reinstating of the death penalty – a stance which is fundamentally different to that of the ANC. The ANC has steadfastly defended the abolishment of the death penalty. It was in 1995 that capital punishment was officially abolished in South Africa by the ruling of the Constitutional Court in the landmark case of *State v Mankwanyane*. The apex court established that capital punishment was inconsistent with the interim constitution's commitment to human rights.

But for the ANC and the progressive left, the death penalty is also a political question – one about the structural and racial inequalities that had always characterised the practice.

However, as argued earlier, crime levels are on the increase, particularly in major cities like Johannesburg. This has resulted in a sense of desperation among ordinary people who believe that not much is being done about the scourge of crime. Young people, who are disproportionately affected by crime, believe in the need for the reinstatement of the death penalty. This was expressed in a 2013 study by consumer insights company Pondering Panda (quoted in SAPA, 2013), which surveyed nearly seven thousand young people across the country, aged between 18 and 34 years. According to the study, 76 percent of the respondents thought that capital punishment should be reinstated, while 80 percent believed that the reinstating would deter criminals and reduce crime.

Mashaba's position on the migrant question also gained popularity with the urban electorate. Mashaba had always linked the issue of crime to that of undocumented immigrants, arguing that these persons were largely responsible for the crime rates in Johannesburg. In an opinion piece published in the Afrikaans newspaper, *Rapport*, Mashaba argued that South Africa's protection of the rights of refugees and migrants should not come at the cost of the country turning its back "on our sovereignty as a democratic state" (quoted in Grobler & AFP, 2019). His reign as Mayor would also be characterised by accusations of xenophobia from civil society groups including the Institute for Race Relations. This was especially pronounced when, in 2018, he made unfounded statements about foreign nationals living in the City of Johannesburg, claiming that 80 percent of people living in the City's hijacked buildings were foreigners – an argument that was disputed by Africa Check (Madisa, 2018)

Understanding Mashaba's politics is crucial in understanding why he was initially immensely popular with the electorate in Johannesburg. It also explains, to a large degree, why the DA believed him to be the best candidate to win them the Black vote, which the party had not always had support from in the city – particularly in its sprawling townships. Mashaba is a populist, but one who is aided by a degree of credibility within the Black community that views him not only as a success story, but also as someone who is genuinely invested in the aspirations of locals, to the exclusion of all other people, who the ANC government always insisted are human beings worthy of regard. It is not difficult to make sense of why the DA would support someone with Mashaba's political background. The party holds Mashaba's views, and while not as brazen as he was in their articulation, the fact that it never distanced itself from them is a clear indication that it sanctioned them. These regressive politics that pathologised Black people and which won him the support of many, would ultimately be the undoing of both Mashaba and the DA-led coalition in the City of Johannesburg.

The short-lived administration of the DA-led coalition was marred with accusations of maladministration. There was poor maintenance of road infrastructure across the City's network and a crisis of waste management. At the launch of its Diphetogo programme, the DA-led coalition laid the blame at the door of the previous ANC-led government. According to Mashaba, the infrastructure problems that the City was experiencing were the result of a metro that had been "run in an environment where corruption was allowed to fester, and neglect of the City's infrastructure was the order of the day" (City of Johannesburg, 2018). He claimed that when they took over government, the DA-led coalition found the City of Johannesburg with an infrastructure backlog of R170 billion (City of Johannesburg, 2018). This would be a response to every problem that confronted his administration: that it was the fault of the previous administration. This sustained lack of responsibility characterised the DA-led coalition in the City of Johannesburg.

However, it would be dishonest to claim that the DA-led coalition did not make some important inroads in addressing some of the City's most salient challenges. The administration invested the largest share of its capital budget in roads, transport, housing, electricity and water, going up from 54 percent in the 2016/17 financial year to 69 percent in the 2018/19 financial year. In addition to this, it set aside R46 million for the acquisition of buildings in the inner city for the purpose of creating affordable housing for residents and R117 million for the electrification of informal settlements. While these are generally responsibilities of municipalities, the DA-led coalition certainly did well to attempt to humanise some of the City's poorest people and communities with these investments in infrastructure and services.

Perhaps the most significant intervention made by Mashaba's administration was the insourcing of more than 1 500 cleaners, who were absorbed into the employ of the municipality in 2019. The cleaners, who used to work for private service providers, were given permanent employment by the City – which came with qualifying for a pension as well as the City's funeral policy, medical aid cover, and subsidised education, among other benefits. This restoration of dignity for the workers was not the result of the DA developing a moral conscience towards the working-class poor (Mashaba would later state, when resigning, that there were people in the DA "who would rather I spent more time on cutting grass than on fixing our broken and aged infrastructure" (Twitter, 2019), an indication that there was great resistance within the party to meaningful infrastructure development that would contribute to broader structural changes for the historically disenfranchised). It was the result of the commitment of the EFF to this struggle which it had initially waged in 2016 in higher learning institutions. The EFF Student Command had been instrumental in the #EndOutsourcing movement that sought to put pressure on universities to permanently employ the cleaning and ground-working staff. The EFF had played an instrumental role in proposing new legislation to end the outsourcing of all government workers at local, provincial, and national level prior to the DA-led coalition doing so in the City of Johannesburg. This is a demonstration of one of the instances where the DA-led administration was steered towards progressive reforms by a strong and ideologically sound coalition partner. There would not be too many.

By 2019, just three years into the coalition, it was becoming evident that the centre could no longer hold. Instability in the two other DA-led metros, Nelson Mandela Bay Metro, and the City of Tshwane, were spilling into the City of Johannesburg. In July of that year, EFF leader Julius Malema threw down the gauntlet, announcing that the EFF would no longer be voting with the DA in all municipalities – including the City of Johannesburg. Malema stated that while the EFF would participate in Council debates and make inputs where necessary, it would abstain from all voting processes. The implications for the DA were catastrophic. In all the metros where it governed through coalitions, the EFF was the kingmaker. A withdrawal of voting support from the EFF, which was effectively withdrawal from the coalition, would render all the Councils hung. Curiously, it had come out that less than a year prior to Malema's announcement, there had been talks within the DA for the party to pull out of coalitions with the EFF. According to De Klerk and Kgosana (2018), a group within the DA had attempted to convince the federal executive to cut ties with the EFF on the basis that the party was prone to threatening the DA whenever there were disagreements within the coalition. Furthermore, the group had argued, Mashaba was readily giving in to the EFF's demands in the City of Johannesburg. According to various interviewees, Mmusi Maimane, who was then the leader of the DA, had tried numerous times to engage Malema and the EFF leadership about staying in the coalition – a plea that would ultimately be disregarded by the EFF leadership almost a year later when it pulled out of the coalition in Nelson Mandela Bay Metro and then later, the City of Johannesburg.

But the collapse of the DA-led coalition in the City was the result of much more than this. According to the former Mayor, who was interviewed for this book, it was funda-mentally about the DA's resistance to meaningful transformation. It was in October 2019, following the election of DA leader Helen Zille as federal council chairperson that it became evident that the DA was not committed to the transformation it had claimed it was. Several interviewees from the DA indicated that the decision to elect Zille was a pushback by a strong conservative grouping within the party, who were uncomfortable with Maimane's position on redress and growing conscientisation around race issues by the largely Black and Coloured membership and leadership. Zille represents the classical liberal values of the DA – values that are sustained by the disregard for the structural nature of racism in South Africa and market fundamentalism. Interestingly, it was the latter that had drawn Mashaba to the DA, but which he would soon realise was incongruent with running a municipality in one of the most unequal cities in the world. Just a few days after Zille's election, Mashaba resigned from the DA and the mayorship of Johannesburg, stating: "The DA no longer represents a party that is able to achieve what I desire most, a movement that can save South Africa, unseat the ANC and deliver one South Africa for all... The election of Helen Zille as the chairperson of the federal council represents a victory for people in the DA who stand diametrically opposed to my beliefs and value system, and I believe those of most South Africans of all backgrounds..." (Feketha, 2019). Mashaba's resignation was followed by those of former DA federal chairperson Athol Trollip and leader, Maimane, who resigned from the organisation and parliament.

The instability within the DA, the decision by the EFF to quit the coalition and Mashaba's resignation resulted in the unravelling of the DA-led coalition in the City of Johannesburg. Following Mashaba's resignation, the EFF fielded its own candidate for the position of Mayor, although it would be the ANC's Geoff Makhubo who would win the election with 137 votes against 101 for the DA's Funzela Ngobeni and 30 for the EFF's Musa Novela. But because the ANC did not win the outright majority required to govern, it too entered a coalition with smaller parties, effectively wrestling the economic hub from the DA-led coalition, which had governed for only three years. Asked about the lessons learned and whether there is a future for coalition governments, the former Mayor of the City of Johannesburg indicated that coalition governments can work if the partners are genuinely committed to the same cause, and that an organisation like the DA is incapable of bringing change precisely because it does not centre the poor. The ANC, he went on to argue, had long betrayed the cause, and what South Africa needs is a new vision – and ethical political leadership.

City of Tshwane

The implosion of the DA-led coalition in the City of Tshwane was perhaps more dramatic than that of the City of Johannesburg. The tensions of the coalition government became so untenable that the Gauteng Provincial Government and courts of law had to intervene to restore stability. The ANC lost the administrative capital to a DA-led coalition in the 2016 local government elections, where the former obtained 41 percent of the vote against the DA's 43 percent. In Tshwane as in the City of Johannesburg, the EFF was the kingmaker, having obtained just over 11 percent of the vote. And while neither of the two dominant parties, the DA and ANC, had the majority vote, it was the DA that was better positioned to form a coalition government. The EFF voted with the DA-led coalition, ensuring that the DA would govern the nation's administrative capital for the first time in the democratic dispensation.

As in the City of Johannesburg, the DA-led coalition in the City of Tshwane did not take too long to implode. In early January 2019, the then mayor of the capital, the DA's Solly Msimanga, announced that he would be resigning to focus on his campaign to become the Premier of the Gauteng Province ahead of the national elections that were set to take place in May of that year. While this was the official explanation given by Msimanga and the DA, interviews conducted with some DA leaders and senior government officials in the Tshwane metro indicated that Msimanga was forced to resign by his party due to unsatisfactory performance and some scandals. These included the appointment of senior officials in his administration who did not meet the minimum requirements for employment by the City. One such person was Marietha Aucamp who was the Chief of Staff in the Mayor's office. Aucamp only had a matric certificate. An investigation instituted by the municipality found that she had lied about her qualifications. Several officials were implicated in her irregular appointment after it was discovered that Human Resource processes in the City had failed to pick up on the falsification of her qualifications. And while the same report cleared Msimanga of any wrongdoing, the matter nonetheless contributed significantly to the growing apprehension on the part of the DA about his mayorship. But perhaps the greatest downfall of both Msimanga and all other DA mayors that came after him in the capital was the GladAfrica tender that haunted the coalition government.

In 2017, the City of Tshwane awarded built environment consultancy firm, GladAfrica, a multi-billion-rand tender to assist the City in the rollout of infrastructure services. Soon thereafter, the Auditor-General released a report that determined that the awarding of the R12 billion tender had been irregular and recommended that the contract be terminated. By then, hundreds of millions had already been paid to the company. Tshwane's City Manager, Moeketsi Mosola, had always insisted that the awarding of the tender was done within regulations and the law, and that a legal opinion had been sought by the City on the matter. The GladAfrica tender imbroglio marked the beginning of the end of the DA-led coalition in the capital, and by the time the contract was cancelled, and the matter resolved, several senior government officials would be gone – as too would Msimanga, under the ostensible reason of focusing on the provincial campaign.

Msimanga's successor, the DA's Stevens Mokgalapa, who was elected by Council in February 2019, would also find himself haunted by the GladAfrica tender scandal. In his inaugural address, Mokgalapa made bold commitments aimed at solidifying his position as an antidote to Msimanga, who was seen by many as ineffective. Among his commitments was that he would ensure that there was an independent forensic investigation unit in the City whose objective would be to investigate any allegations of wrongdoing or corruption. Speaking directly to the GladAfrica problem, Mokgalapa indicated that he would improve consequence management in the City and ensure that recommendations of forensic investigations and reports of the Auditor-General were implemented. Within weeks in office, Mokgalapa managed to cancel the controversial GladAfrica tender – a move that confirmed his self-proclaimed status as "Mr Service Delivery".

A few months following this, Mosola stepped down and was replaced by Moeketsi Ntsimane, who became the Acting City Manager under Mokgalapa. Ntsimane was in the position for only three months, being mired in a similar scandal as that which had eclipsed Msimanga's administration: the appointment of an unqualified senior official. This time, Previn Govender, the former head of Tshwane Emergency Services, was appointed without the requisite qualifications – an appointment that Ntsimane defended even as contrary evidence was provided, including findings by the Public Protector, Advocate Busisiwe Mkhwebane, that the appointment was irregular and needed to be set aside. According to the Public Protector's report, "The salary paid to Govender from

August 2017 to date constitutes unlawful enrichment as he was not qualified for appointment in the post of chief of emergency... In the circumstances, I find that the appointment of Mr Govender in the post of chief of emergency was irregular, unlawful, and thus constituted improper conduct as envisaged by section 182(1)(a) of the Constitution, 1996, and maladministration as envisaged by section 6(4)(a)(i) of the Public Protector Act,1994" (Public Protector, 2020). As part of her remedial action, the Public Protector requested that the Member of the Executive Committee (MEC) for Cooperative Governance and Traditional Affairs (COGTA), Lebogang Maile, consider the report, and where appropriate take steps within fourteen days to remedy the maladministration and improper conduct identified therein. Ntsimane and Govender left the City soon thereafter.

A year following his election, Mokgalapa was also forced to resign as the Executive Mayor. In January 2020, a ruinous recording of Mokgalapa and then Member of the Mayoral Committee (MMC) for Transport and Roads, Sheila Senkubuge, engaged in sexual intercourse in a municipal office, was released. Beyond the ethical questions that the tape raised, on it, the former Executive Mayor of the administrative capital could be heard communicating plans to fire senior government officials and speaking ill of political leaders in the metro. Mokgalapa was immediately placed on special leave by the DA, with DA Tshwane leader Abel Tau appointed as the Acting Executive Mayor while an investigation into Mokgalapa and Senkubuge's conduct was underway. Within days, the Senkubuge resigned and opposition parties, as well as the EFF, called for the removal of Mokgalapa. At the conclusion of the investigation, he was forced to resign as the Executive Mayor of the City of Tshwane and in October 2020, he announced his resignation from the DA. This means that within four years of assuming office, the DA-led coalition in Tshwane had elected two Executive Mayors and appointed one Acting Executive Mayor. The revolving-door administration also saw several senior officials including a City Manager and Acting City Manager, removed.

A senior administrator who was interviewed for this book claimed that Msimanga was the sacrificial lamb in what was effectively a battle between the ANC and EFF for the control of the capital's purse. According to this official, it was the EFF through the City Manager that was intricately linked to the GladAfrica tender. Evidence of this is given in the motion of no confidence against Msimanga that was put by the EFF shortly before Msimanga's resignation, and the party's passionate support for Mosola, who was at the centre of the multi-billion-rand tender. While still the Executive Mayor, Msimanga had tried on numerous occasions to have Mosola fired – but had failed. A senior official in the City argued that it was this that led to tensions between the DA-coalition and the EFF – that the former saw the EFF's support for Mosola as an attempt at undermining the coalition and flexing its muscle as a reminder of its kingmaker status. The three-year battle between Msimanga and Mosola (who would later concede with the Auditor-General that the GladAfrica contract was indeed irregular) provides an important glimpse into the subject of the politics-administration interface.

Maserumule (2007) analyses the chronic phenomenon of conflict between Ministers and their Directors-General, arguing that it could pose an impediment to the delivery of public services. While in this context the conflict was between the Executive Mayor and the City Manager, the same postulations could be made about the causes of the conflict, albeit with some new insights specific to the City of Tshwane coalition context. Maserumule's contention that such conflict thwarts service delivery was evidenced in Tshwane where the legacy of the battle between Executive Mayors and City Managers occurred. Later when the capital would be placed under administration by the Gauteng Provincial Government, Premier Makhura would make the same observations as Maserumule, stating: "The city is not just leaderless, it is rudderless. There is no direction, there is no service delivery in the city. The current uncertainty, instability, inaction and collapse of service delivery must be confronted fearlessly and stopped in its tracks..." (Mailovich, 2020).

While no corroborating evidence of the claims of Mosola's clandestine relations with the EFF was provided by the interviewee as well as those who blew the lid on the tender, including the Young Communist League (YCL) in the Tshwane district, it became an accepted narrative that painted not just the DA-led coalition corrupt and unethical, but the EFF as a co-conspirator in the matter. It is both important and curious to note that while the YCL in Tshwane was instrumental in putting pressure on the City to fire Mosola, who would eventually step down in July 2019, it was also vocal in its scathing criticism of the regional leadership of the ANC. In an opinion piece published in the *Pretoria News*, the former District Secretary of the YCL in Tshwane made this telling statement: "It now appears that the ANC has changed its tune, and where once it was at the forefront of exposing the corruption in the metro as facilitated by the Big Man [Moeketsi Mosola], it has since focused all its energies on Msimanga while remaining eerily silent on the accounting officer that is throwing the city into Armageddon. This necessarily begs the question: why has the ANC, once vocal about the Big Man's role in the systematic collapse of the metro, undergone a Damascene conversion?" (Morifi, 2019). This demonstrated the tensions within components of the mass democratic movement, which, alarmingly, were also at the heart of what led to the ANC's loss of power in Tshwane.

The placing of the City of Tshwane under administration by the provincial government was an inevitable response to what had evidently become an untenable political situation. In early March 2020, the Gauteng Premier, David Makhura, announced that the metro would be placed under administration following months of political wrangling between the DA, EFF and ANC, which had severely impacted the functioning of government. By this time, the EFF had withdrawn its support for the DA-led coalition, resulting in a situation where Council could not reach agreement on any legislative issues. In the months leading to the metro being placed under administration, Council meetings could also not quorate as both the ANC and EFF would often not participate. In addition to this, following the departure of Mosola and Ntsimane, the Acting City Manager who succeeded him was also subsequently removed after only three months in the position, and the metro found itself without a City Manager. The resignation of Mokgalapa also resulted in the City not having a Mayor. What this meant was that the administrative capital was without any executive or accounting authority, making it impossible for it to function, as without leadership, there could be no delivery of services or meaningful administration of the metro. This had led to a series of protests in the City, one of which was the protest by municipal workers over a demand for benchmarking of payments, which the City was unable to facilitate due to constrained finances. This had led to problems of waste management at a time when the country was battling a global pandemic. Additionally, one of the consequences of protest action had been suspension of ward-based out-reach focusing on screening and testing for COVID-19. Under these circumstances, it is evident why the provincial government had seen it necessary to invoke section 139 of the Constitution, which placed the City under administration. The political conditions not only made governance extremely difficult, but people's lives were placed at risk.

But in keeping with the conflicts within the metro, the DA challenged the decision in court, arguing that the provincial government's decision to dissolve the Council was politically motivated and that it was procedurally unfair and irrational. A month after the City was placed under administration, the North Gauteng High Court overturned the provincial government's decision, with costs. In addition to overturning the decision, the court also found that EFF and ANC councillors kept breaking quorum deliberately, making it impossible for the Council to take decisions and effectively govern, and thus forcing its dissolution. The two parties were instructed to attend Council meetings. The administrators that had been appointed by the provincial government were permit-ted to exercise powers conferred upon them for another week, after which the DA-led coalition was expected to continue governing the metro. In October 2020, six months after the court's decision, the City of Tshwane elected a new Mayor, the DA's Randall Williams. Despite this, the challenges of service delivery that informed the provincial government's decision to place the City under administration persist, with the billing crisis, refuse removal and the water crisis in Hammanskraal persisting.

The challenges of the DA-led coalition in Tshwane, while a focal point of this argument, must also be understood as a by-product of the ANC's failure to win the metro. As a senior ANC official said to me in an interview for this book, to understand the coalition politics of Tshwane it would be important to understand how and why the ANC's internal battles contributed to the party's loss of power in the metro. In June 2016, several areas across the Tshwane metro were caught in violent protests resulting from news that Thoko Didiza would be the mayoral candidate for the metro, replacing then Regional Chairperson and Mayor, Kgosientso "Sputla" Ramokgopa. On 18 June 2016, the ANC named mayoral candidates for all municipalities in Gauteng and the then former Minister who had served in President Thabo Mbeki's cabinet was named a candidate for the

City of Tshwane. Within a day of this announcement, members of the ANC took to the streets in protest, arguing that the provincial leadership had not consulted branches on the decision. There was a strong sentiment that Sputla, whose administration had been hailed as innovative and effective, should serve a second term. Another faction within the organisation preferred the then Regional Secretary, Mapiti Matsena, to take over the reins. The previous Regional Congress had also been punctuated by the extraordinarily bitter contestation between a faction supporting the two key political players in the Tshwane region. The battle for the mayoral candidacy was thus a continuation of what had begun as a battle within the organisation – demonstrating the complex ways in which the party and the state become enmeshed in each other's politics.

Didiza's proposed candidacy was met with not just political difference, but also, political violence. In the wake of the announcement of her candidacy, violence flared up across the metro, with protests taking place in the city centre as well as township areas. There was serious vandalism of property and the blocking of several streets, preventing traffic flow and impacting economic activity within the City. So significant was the threat of sustained violence that the ANC provincial leadership had to make interventions that included visiting areas where the violence was most pronounced. These interventions did not have the desired outcomes. One ANC member who attended a meeting in Atteridgeville that was called by the provincial leadership with an NEC member and Sputla in tow, explained how attendants rejected the idea of Sputla being replaced. The meeting at which there was heavy political presence, was unable to convince ANC members to support Didiza, and according to the interviewee, shouts of "No Sputla, no vote" that had been made since the announcement of Didiza's candidacy were passionately repeated by the crowd. The meeting was reported by Maromo (2016) as having been extremely tense. The sentiment that without Sputla there would be massive withholding of votes was so strong that according to ANC Tshwane regional leaders interviewed, it shaped the outcome of the elections.

The tensions around the mayoral candidate for the City of Tshwane laid bare the extent to which the ANC was fractured. The complete disregard by the party's members for the political wisdom of the provincial leadership that agreed on the name of Didiza pointed to a profoundly serious breakdown of trust and communication, without which the organisation could not have mounted a successful electoral campaign. But it was not only the ANC that was impacted – the issue also impacted relations within the tripartite alliance as lines were drawn that would continue to exist long after the elections had passed. That these unresolved tensions impacted the organisation in the region is not conjecture but is evidenced by the divisions within the regional leadership that exist today and were highlighted even as the ANC sat in opposition benches in Council. The road to the 2016 local government elections in the City of Tshwane was paved with discontent from which the organisation is yet to recover, and the discontent has the potential to affect the upcoming 2021 local government elections that find the ANC on a backfoot.

Nelson Mandela Bay Metropolitan Municipality

The ANC's loss of power in the Nelson Mandela Bay Metro was perhaps the most expected. It had been evident for a while leading up to the 2016 local government elections that the party was bleeding significantly, and that the social contract between the voters and the organisation's leadership in government had been broken irremediably. The DA received 47.7 percent of the vote against the ANC's 41.79 percent (IEC, 2016). The EFF won 5.23 percent of the vote. As with the metros in the Gauteng Province, while the DA had most of the votes, it did not win an outright majority and therefore needed to establish a coalition to govern. The EFF was once again placed in a unique and powerful position to swing the vote, and it opted to vote with the DA, bringing to four the number of metros in the country that were under a DA-led administration at the end of the election run (the City of Cape Town had been and remains under a majority DA government).

As with all elections, independent surveys and polls were conducted by various institutions to gauge the attitudes and thinking of voters. Just a week prior to the elections, the most credible of these, the Ipsos poll, had indicated that the DA mayoral candidate Athol Trollip remained far more popular than ANC mayoral candidate Danny Jordaan (eNCA, 2016). This came as no surprise as the ANC had, for years before the elections, been battling with reputational issues arising from the endless accusations against the municipal administration for maladministration, misappropriation of state resources and corruption. Among these was the Integrated Public Transport System project that has haunted the metro. Back in 2010, the Nelson Mandela Bay Metro was among those selected for a rapid bus system and the Integrated Public Transport System (IPTS) project was administered with funding allocated by the National Treasury. Shortly thereafter, the metro undertook another major project – the Implementation and Maintenance of an Institutional Contracts Management and Administration System (ICMAS). These two projects would be at the centre of Hawks investigations when, in 2014, an audit report by the National Treasury indicated that they were mired in irregularities and gross inflation of prices. The issue brought to the surface major problems for the ANC government in the metro. For one thing, the challenges with the IPTS led to serious standoffs between the municipality and the powerful taxi industry. Secondly, the matter of a syndicate running the municipality was cemented by the Hawks investigation.

According to the Hawks, there existed in the Nelson Mandela Bay municipality a syndicate of businessmen and ANC politicians that was deeply embedded in the affairs of government. The syndicate operated with common purpose to unlawfully circumvent the prescribed procurement processes to benefit specific suppliers or consultants irregularly and fraudulently. The South African Government News Agency reported at the time that the investigation indicated that influential office bearers colluded with municipal officials and controlled decision-making in the appointments of specific persons in critical municipal posts. This was purportedly done to influence procurement processes as well as the appointments of entities willing to advance the interests of the syndicate. The alleged objective was to ensure a steady stream of unlawful payments from the Municipality to members of the syndicate where the funds were distributed to other syndicate members. The National Treasury report and subsequent Hawks investigation laid the foundation for more corruption scandals within the metro to be revealed, leading ultimately to intervention from the national Department of Cooperative Governance and Traditional Affairs with then Minister Pravin Gordhan deploying Crispian Olver to root out the corruption in the municipality to redeem the ANC-led government. Olver, a former senior government official, would later write a book, *How to Steal a City: The Battle for Nelson Mandela Bay*, detailing his experiences with the municipality, confirming the allegations communicated by the Hawks, and exposing the shocking depths to which the malaise in Nelson Mandela Bay metro went.

In addition to the corruption scandals that plagued the municipality, there was also the matter of political killings that had not until that point been associated with the politics of the region or the broader Eastern Cape Province. In August 2014, Councillor Buyisile Mkavu, who at the time was serving as the MMC for Housing, was assassinated in Kwanobuhle, a township on the outskirts of Port Elizabeth. Mkavu was shot multiple times and died at the scene (*The Herald*, 2014). Mkavu had been extremely critical of corruption in the metro and since his deployment, had been looking into various irregular housing projects and transactions within his department. Among these was the Missionvale housing development, a large-scale low-cost housing development that was funded through a grant that had been decentralised to the metro municipality. Mkavu did an investigation of this housing development and it picked up a significant number of irregularities relating to the competency of the contractor who was awarded the tender as well as the quality of the houses. *The Herald* (2016) would later report that the houses were built without the internal reticulation being done and were without running water, sewage disposal facilities or electricity. Mkavu had compiled a dossier of evidence of the numerous instances of corruption and irregularities with contracts in his department and, a week prior to his assassination, had presented it to the Mayoral committee with hopes of being enabled to remove some senior key officials.

The assassination of Mkavu had a profoundly serious impact on the politics of the metro. It has been stated that: "The political murder cast a pall over the whole of Port Elizabeth... there was a noticeable climate of fear... Corruption in the administration... had become entrenched to such an extent that the ruling ANC was facing a massive loss of electoral support. Everyone spoke about it, but most were clearly anxious for their own safety, and spoke only carefully in private rooms and corners. At Mkavu's memorial service the Speaker of Council, Maria Hermans, confessed: "some of us live in fear and uncertainty because we don't know who's going to be next". Many had retreated from open contestation with the corrupt forces that operated in the city, but behind closed doors they would open up and talk about these untouchable, larger than life characters that operated across the municipality. Some felt that corruption was intractable; that the leadership of the metro was heavily implicated and hence incapable of acting against it" (Olver, 2016).

All these problems and more had a bearing on the ANC's electoral performance. The party saw a significant decline in the 2014 general elections where it obtained only 49 percent of the local vote – far below the national vote of 62 percent. It represented the second-lowest electoral support for the party, second only to the City of Cape Town that was under a DA-led government. This decline in electoral support was already evident in the growing number of service delivery protests over time. According to Joleen Steyn Kotze, Associate Professor of Politics at the Nelson Mandela University in Port Elizabeth, by 2012, protests in Nelson Mandela Bay had escalated to such a degree that the Eastern Cape Province was dubbed the "protest-ridden province" (The Conversation, 2016). In addition to this, the protests had become increasingly violent. According to doctoral research conducted on the causes of service delivery protests in Nelson Mandela Bay Metro, there were a myriad of factors at play, some which were causally linked to deployment issues within the governing party. The Strategic Political Advisor: Policy, Research and Planning in the Office of the Executive Mayor who was interviewed for the study posited that the root causes of service delivery protests lie in a number of factors including "the growing social distance between the elected representatives and the com-munities that Councillors are supposed to serve; poor communication; incapacity on the side of elected politicians to understand the complexity of the issues they have to deal with as a result of misdeployment; and… policy failure on the part of government" (Shaidi, 2013).

An interesting dynamic that was highlighted by Kotze pertains to the role of the National Union of Metalworkers of South Africa (NUMSA) in the declining support of the ANC in the Bay metro. The motor industry in Nelson Mandela Bay metro is huge. The metro's economy is primarily oriented towards automotive assembly, manufacturing, and export industries, with the Volkswagen, Ford and General Motors plants located there, among others. The FAW Group Corporation, a Chinese state-owned automotive manufacturing company, has also built a multi-billion-rand plant in the region. Most other industries are geared towards the motor vehicle industry, providing parts such as wiring harnesses, catalytic converters, batteries and tyres to the vehicle manufacturers. Most unionised workers in the metro belong to NUMSA, which in 2014, was expelled from COSATU. It is important to note that prior to its expulsion, it was the largest affiliate of the trade union federation that is part of the tripartite alliance with the ANC. NUMSA is also the single biggest trade union in South Africa. As of January 2014, the union had 339 567 members (NUMSA website). In 2013 following a special national congress, NUMSA took the decision to withdraw support for the ANC and the SACP and indicated that it would not support the governing party (or any other party) for the general elections the following year (George, 2013). It was expelled from COSATU soon thereafter. According to Kotze (2016), this had an impact on the support for the ANC in the Nelson Mandela Bay metro where NUMSA had significant political muscle. This may have had a direct impact on the party's 2014 electoral performance and subsequent decline in voter support.

It was evident, leading up to the 2016 local government elections, that the ANC-led government in the Bay Metro was in serious trouble. While most of the problems seemed to be with the municipality, they were in fact a product of factional battles and tensions within the organisation and broadly, the tripartite alliance, as indicated with the NUMSA/COSATU debacle. These tensions came to a head on the eve of the elections when members of the ANC took to the streets protesting the list of candidates for Councillors. According to members from eight wards in the metro, the provincial leadership of the party had sought to impose candidates on the branches, resulting in the protests that culminated in members of the Regional Executive Committee being held hostage by the protesting members (*The Herald*, 2016). The political tensions were slightly eased by the decision of the provincial executive to resubmit its Councillor candidate list, citing as the reason for the conflict that: "There were issues like duplication. Some issues are in relation to the popular candidates versus the candidates recommended by the committees" (Sesant, 2016). However, by this time, not only had divisions within the party been cemented, but there was also growing sentiment among voters that they would not participate in the elections or would vote for the opposition.

The ANC was punished by voters at the polls, resulting in the DA forming a coalition government that included several smaller parties comprising the Congress of the People (COPE), the African Christian Democratic Party (ACDP) and General Bantu Holomisa's United Democratic Movement (UDM), which would later play a significant role in the coalition government. Seasoned DA leader Athol Trollip, who at the time was serving as the Federal Chairperson of the party, was elected as the Executive Mayor of the Nelson Mandela Bay metro. While Trollip's brief administration has often been applauded for bringing a degree of economic stability in the metro, culminating in a rating's upgrade from Moody's due to the municipality's persistently low debt levels and strong liquidity profile relative to its counterparts in the country (Paulse, 2018), tensions within the coalition government, specifically between Trollip and his deputy, the UDM's Mongameli Bobani, were deeply pronounced. According to Trollip, the root of this conflict was corruption on the part of Bobani, who was allegedly irate when the DA-led coalition administration in the Bay metro stopped the payments of several contracts. This resulted in Bobani beginning to vote against the DA in Council, contravening the coalition agreement. Addressing the Cape Town Press Club in 2018 shortly after being removed as the Executive Mayor, Trollip alleged that he had evidence that the UDM had taken dirty money to fund its 2016 electoral campaign, and that Holomisa had known about a string of criminal acts that Bobani had committed but was unwilling to act. This, he claimed, had been one of the areas of conflict within the DA-led coalition: the fact that while the DA was hard at work trying to rid the Bay metro of corruption, its coalition partner was engaged in it.

In May 2017, the DA-led coalition took the decision to remove Bobani from the coalition government. Bobani was serving in Trollip's Mayoral Committee as the MMC for Public Health. Just three months later, the Patriotic Alliance brought a motion of no confidence against Bobani, seeking to remove him as the Deputy Executive Mayor. The vote on the motion proceeded without Bobani and opposition parties, who had staged a walkout. Despite this, it passed. Bobani and the UDM filed an urgent application to have the vote of no confidence set aside, but the Eastern Cape High Court dismissed the application with costs on the basis that it was not urgent (Spies, 2017). The UDM's motion had been supported by a significant number of Council members as well as the metro's administrators including the City Manager. Following the court's ruling, the UDM officially withdrew from the DA-led coalition and was immediately replaced by the Patriotic Alliance that had brought the motion against Bobani. Bobani's position in the Mayoral Committee was filled by the ACDP.

The removal of Bobani marked the beginning of the end for Trollip. According to several people interviewed for this book, it cemented the idea that the DA was a racist White party that was unwilling to work with Black people unless it could dominate them. This sentiment would become dominant across all the metros and would undermine the DA's assertions that it was a party that is invested in transformation and the celebration of diversity. The DA's actions, and the sentiment that it was racist, also created tensions with the EFF, which a few months later, announced that it would remove Trollip as the Executive Mayor of Nelson Mandela Bay (Areff, 2018). The EFF's decision had been informed by the DA's decision to reject the EFF's motion to allow a constitutional review on land expropriation without compensation. While this motion had been made at the National Assembly, the EFF argued that it would not continue to support a DA that had demonstrated disregard for a motion that would bring about meaningful transformation for the Black majority of South Africa. The EFF's motion had been supported by the majority of parties at the National Assembly, including the ANC. This point is extremely important given the historically hostile relations between the ANC and the EFF, because it demonstrates that when push comes to shove, the two parties can find convergence on issues of importance for Black people.

In August 2018, exactly two years since the formation of the DA-led coalition in the Nelson Mandela Bay metro, Trollip was removed through a motion of no confidence brought by opposition parties and a DA Councillor, Mbulelo Manyati. Trollip's removal followed on the heels of the removal of the DA's Speaker of Council, Jonathan Lawack, who had also been removed with the help of Manyati. In that instance, Manyati had abstained from voting, ensuring that the motion would pass with just a single vote. While his membership was subsequently terminated by the DA, the ousting of the Speaker and Executive Mayor would stand. In a move aimed at undermining the DA's authority in the metro, the Council voted for Bobani as Trollip's replacement, effectively wrestling away power from the DA-led coalition. A DA leader who was interviewed for this book stated that the move had been psychologically bruising for Trollip and the DA, and that it had led to serious panic in the organisation as it had become clear that the EFF had played an instrumental role in the outcome. This, he indicated, did not bode well for the party given that it had greater numerical power in the other metros – the City of Johannesburg and the City of Tshwane – and could thus remove the DA there too. These fears would prove prophetic when just a few months later, the EFF would play an instrumental role in the destabilisation of the said metros, leading to resignations by their Mayors.

Just as Bobani had attempted when he was removed from Trollip's Mayoral Committee, the DA filed an urgent application to declare Bobani's election null and void and return Trollip to the position. But the Eastern Cape High Court dismissed the application, arguing that Manyati, who had voted with the opposition to remove Trollip, had been a legitimate councillor until he resigned. This enabled Bobani to constitute his Mayoral Committee, which comprised of ANC leaders including Andile Lungisa, a popular ANC figure in the Bay region. Bobani, like Mokgalapa in the Tshwane metro, would serve only a year in his position. His mayorship was fraught with allegations of corruption, maladministration, and under-performance. The National Treasury also raised concerns over "alleged interference in supply chain management procedures" in Bobani's admin-istration (*News24*, 2018). One of the projects in which Bobani was linked to corruption had been the Integrated Public Transport System which I mentioned earlier as having been mired in controversies of corruption under the ANC-led government prior to the 2016 local government elections. The DA pursued a criminal case against Bobani and in April 2019, his residence and Mayoral offices were raided in connection with tender fraud – a development that greatly embarrassed the coalition government although it stood by him. A member of the metro's Council who was interviewed for this book stated that Bobani had been an unfit Executive Mayor, but that they had voted for him as the ANC only because it would ensure the removal of a DA Mayor.

During his tenure, Bobani had a total of six motions of no confidence brought against him – surviving five of them. But he was eventually voted out in December 2019 after DA Councillor Morne Steyn's motion found the support of the majority of parties in the Council, which included the Patriotic Alliance, ACDP, COPE, AIC, ANC and the DA (Kimberley & Nkosi, 2019). The Bay metro found itself in the same situation as the City of Tshwane of having to appoint an Acting Mayor while back-and-forth legal proceedings were underway. Thsonono Buyeye of the AIC became the Acting Mayor and curiously, in August 2020, he appointed Bobani to the position of MMC for Infrastructure and Engineering. But by November, it was becoming evident that the Nelson Mandela Bay metro was on the brink of collapse. The instability had resulted in a severe crisis of failure to deliver services. In October of that year, the National Treasury had withheld crucial grants amounting to R1.6 billion (Nkosi, 2020). These were meant to subsidise the metro's most destitute residents in the time of the COVID-19 pandemic but due to the municipality having no Mayor and the broader political instabilities that resulted in non-compliance with guidelines, the National Treasury could not release the funds. This resulted in the Eastern Cape Provincial government raising concerns that it could dissolve the metro and place it under administration. This would have been the second time that a metro municipality in a coalition-government would have been placed under administration following the situation in the City of Tshwane.

In November 2020, the Grahamstown High Court issued an order that the Speaker of Council call a special meeting to elect a new Executive Mayor within a week. In December 2020, DA Councillor Nqaba Bhanga was elected as the Executive Mayor, bringing an end to the political instability but not so much to service delivery, which had suffered immeasurably during the period of conflict in the DA-led coalition government, creating a significant backlog. The DA-led coalition in the Nelson Mandela Bay metro went through three elected Executive Mayors and one Acting Mayor. The people who bore the brunt of this instability were the residents of the metro who had crucial funds withheld from them by the National Treasury and had services halted. The Bay metro, like the City of Tshwane, is a vivid representation of what happens when a coalition government collapses. It leads to disruptions in governance, which in turn impact on the lives of ordinary people and in many cases, the violation of their basic human rights, as was the case with the water crisis in Hammanskraal.

It is important to note that Bhanga cut his political teeth in the Congress movement, having served as the Regional Chairperson of the Congress of South African Students (COSAS), the Secretary General of the South African Students Congress (SASCO) and a regional leader of the ANC Youth League, before joining COPE, which came into being as a result of a split from the ANC following the contentious removal of former President Thabo Mbeki. This point is raised to demonstrate how conflicts in the ANC benefit opposition parties not only in terms of electoral votes, but also in weakening its qualitative capacity. That disunity within the party and not so much support for the opposition, specifically the DA, is the main cause of the ANC's electoral decline is not conjecture, and the case of Metsimaholo Local Municipality, which I will touch on next, as well as instances where ANC Councillors voted to remove Mayors, is the evidence.

*On 30 September 2020, Mongameli Bobani was approached for an interview by myself and my research team. We agreed to a virtual meeting within the coming week, and he was very keen to participate in the interview. On the same day, we emailed him the list of questions that we would be asking him. Unfortunately, he was hospitalised soon after our brief discussion and subsequently passed away due to COVID-19-related complications in November 2020. May his soul rest in peace.

Metsimaholo Local Municipality

Towards the 2016 local government elections, there had been great focus on Metsimaholo Local Municipality located in the Fezile Dabi District Municipality in northern Free State Province. The third largest of the four local municipalities in the district (the others being Moqhaka, Ngwathe and Mafube local municipalities), Metsimaholo, became the site of one of the toughest battles for political power in democratic South Africa – and a symbol of the tensions within the Congress Movement. In the 2016 local government elections, the ANC won 41 percent of the vote against the DA's 29 percent, the EFF's 17.9 percent, the Metsimaholo Community Association's (MCA) 4.9 percent, and the Freedom Front Plus's 2.1 percent (Independent Electoral Commission, 2016). As no party had won an outright majority, this resulted in a hung Council, necessitating the formation of a coalition government. The EFF was once again in the unique position of being the kingmaker, and as in all other metros, opted to support the DA. The coalition government, which comprised of all the opposition parties, was thus established in Metsimaholo, hurling the ANC into opposition benches for the first time in the local municipality. The MCA's Sello Hlasa was elected as Mayor while the DA's Arnoldi du Plooy took the position of Speaker of Council.

The story of Metsimaholo cannot be understood without understanding the history of the MCA. The MCA was established in 2013 as a pressure group opposing the national government's proposed amalgamation of Metsimaholo and the neighbouring Ngwathe Local Municipality. The Free State provincial government had made a submission to the Department of Co-operative Governance and Traditional Affairs proposing the merger, but it was fiercely rejected by communities across Metsimaholo. In January 2013, residents of Zamdela, a township in Sasolburg, the seat of the Metsimaholo Local Municipality, took to the streets to protest the proposed amalgamation (Hlahla, 2013). Burning tyres, barricaded roads, vandalism of property and looting characterised the protests. Residents of Zamdela argued that the former Premier of the province, Ace Magashule, was behind the proposed merger based on him being from Parys, a town in the Ngwathe Local Municipality that, according to the protesters, was notorious for bad service delivery and colossal debt owed to Eskom (Xaba, 2013). To understand this history, which is crucial to understanding why the ANC lost Metsimaholo, my research team visited Sasolburg in 2020 to speak to individuals who had participated in the protests. They indicated that the provincial government had not consulted them adequately on the proposed merger and that even when they submitted their objections to the Municipal Demarcation Board, there still seemed to be an insistence on the part of the provincial government to proceed with the amalgamation. One of the people interviewed stated that the ANC's Brutus Mahlaku, who was the Mayor of Metsimaholo, seemed oblivious to the objections of the people of Sasolburg, and had continued to insist that the demarcation was in accordance with processes of the demarcation board and would be in the best interests of the residents of Metsimaholo Local Municipality.

This, the interviewees stated, was indicative of a government that was deaf to the demands of the people and therefore a government that needed to be punished.

In August 2013, the Municipal Demarcation Board withdrew its proposal to amalgamate Ngwathe and Metsimaholo Local Municipalities, but by this time, the MCA had gained political support throughout Metsimaholo. The association had established a strong community presence and was beginning to take up popular struggles and issues of service delivery. A key figure who helped establish the MCA informed my research team that many of the people who participated in the organisation were in fact members or supporters of the ANC, and that the organisation had sought only to hold the party accountable for some of its political decisions including the proposed amalgamation. The organisation's decision to contest the 2016 local government elections, he insisted, was the result not so much of wanting to remove the ANC from power but wanting to create pressure from within government. The MCA thus gained an opportunity to be part of government when, in 2016, it entered a coalition with the DA, the Freedom Front Plus, and the EFF.

The MCA, DA, EFF and Freedom Front Plus coalition did not last even six months. By January 2017, tensions had begun to rise between the coalition partners, with the DA arguing that Hlasa had failed to comply with the coalition's strategic plan, had also not submitted the 100 days report and had misused state resources. The conflict culminated in a proposed motion of a no confidence vote against Hlasa, scheduled for 31 January 2017. However, it was later postponed to give Hlasa the opportunity to respond to the allegations levelled against him. In early February of that year, an ANC Councillor resigned, leaving a vacancy. The by-election laid bare the conflict within the coalition, with the MCA supporting the ANC candidate. The ANC retained the ward. By the end of that month, Hlasa had reshuffled his Mayoral Committee, replacing it with ANC members. A member of the MCA explained to my research team that the community of Metsimaholo, with whom the MCA had remained in constant communication, had given the party the mandate to work with the ANC as the community did not trust the DA and its coalition partners. A DA leader in Sasolburg who was interviewed for this book refuted these claims, arguing that the MCA had from the very beginning been keen on working with the ANC, and that the differences between the two parties (the MCA and ANC) were nothing more than "sibling rivalry". The DA, he contended, was used by the MCA, which was never genuine in its commitments to the coalition.

Following the reconstitution of the Mayoral Committee by Hlasa, the DA-coalition indicated that it would table a motion of no confidence against him. But this would have been futile because the DA, EFF and Freedom Front coalition had 21 seats in the Council (12 from the DA, eight from the EFF and one from the Freedom Front Plus) – the exact number that the ANC and MCA also had when combined (19 from the ANC and 2 from the MCA). The re-alignment of the coalition resulted in a hung Council. The highly divided

Council battled to govern the municipality and when it failed to adopt a budget for the 2017/2018 financial year, the provincial government stepped in and dissolved it. This was in line with section 139(4) of the Constitution, which states that if a municipality does not approve a budget, the relevant provincial executive must intervene and take appropriate steps, including the dissolving of the Municipal Council and the appointment of an administrator. As such, an administrator was appointed, and by-elections were scheduled for November of 2017.

The by-elections were highly contested, with national leaders from some parties including the DA and EFF descending upon the Free State municipality to campaign. Of significance was the decision of the South African Communist Party to participate in the by-election. The ANC and DA both retained the wards that they had previously won, albeit both suffering a decline in voter support. Out of the sixteen wards retained by the ANC, only three were won by over 50 percent compared to the previous year's municipal elections when it received 50 percent voter support in 15 wards of the wards. The party gained 16 seats, down from 19 in the 2016 elections. The DA gained 11 seats, one less than it had previously won. The EFF maintained the same number of seats, at eight, as did the Freedom Front Plus, with one seat, although with a significant increase of over two percent compared to the previous elections. The MCA, which had played a crucial role in the 2016 elections, saw a significant decline in voter support. Its percentage dropped from 4.91 percent to 1.48 percent, resulting in the loss of one of its initial two seats. Three parties made impressive forays into Metsimaholo. The African Independent Congress (AIC) won a PR seat and 2.11 percent of the vote; the Forum for Service Delivery (F4SD) won a seat and the SACP won three seats.

Important issues arose from the by-elections. The first was that the ANC was on a downward spiral, haemorrhaging support at unprecedented levels. The results of the elections indicated that the party had lost voters to the EFF as well as the SACP. The Party had an impressive showing in their first electoral contest and came remarkably close to winning Ward 3 where the ANC beat them by only 34 votes, obtaining 35 percent of the vote compared to the Party's 34 percent. And while the ANC obtained less than 50 percent of the votes in 15 of the 16 wards that it won, the Party was able to garner over 10 percent of the vote in six of the 16 wards that the ANC won. Another important issue relates to the increased support for the Freedom Front Plus, which evidently took votes from the DA. It is important to remember that the Metsimaholo by-elections took place while Mmusi Maimane was still the leader of the DA, in which there was a strong sentiment among some that the party was becoming invested in race politics. According to Feketha (2019), Helen Zille had been one of those who openly questioned the DA's direction under Maimane as she viewed it as "going south" and moving away from its classical liberal values. The Institute of Race Relations, where Zille has worked as a senior fellow before returning to Chair the Federal Executive, had also expressed concerns about the party's policy posture and called for the removal of Maimane and his replacement with a White leader (Feketha, 2019). The loss of DA votes to the Freedom Front Plus corroborates the view that had been expressed by the EFF when it ceased its relations with DA-led coalitions that the party was a convergence point of racists who were resistant to change.

Following the by-elections, Metsimaholo once again found itself with a hung Council as none of the parties had won an outright majority. This time, however, the ANC was able to regain control of the local municipality by forming a coalition government with the MCA and all the newcomers to the Council, namely, the SACP, the AIC and the F4SD. Lindiwe Tshongwe of the SACP was elected as the Mayor, the ANC's Thabo Kenneth Mabasa as the Speaker of Council, and the MCA's Mashia Vuyo Lennox as the Council Whip. The Mayoral Committee was also formed with representatives from all coalition partners. Following the establishment of the ANC-led coalition, Metsimaholo went through a very brief period of relative stability, with service delivery resuming after a period of wrangling and dissolution of Council. However, in February 2021, Tshongwe was facing a motion of no confidence brought on by the DA. Importantly, towards the date of the scheduled motion, the ANC in the municipality was not throwing its support behind her, with the party's Chief Whip, Lukaas Fischer, stating that she had failed to deal with the key issues plaguing the municipality (Ledwaba, 2021). And although the motion would ultimately be halted due to procedural issues, it exposed the extent to which the divisions within the ANC-led alliance persist.

Reflections from Other Political Developments in the Country

While this submission is about realities and the future of coalition governments following the 2016 local government elections, it would be amiss not to reflect on other political developments that have happened or are happening in other local and district municipalities where the ANC is confronted with significant political crises that beg for reflection. A contention has been made throughout this book that the most immediate threat to the party's hegemony is not just the evolving nature of politics but divisions within the organisation. As demonstrated in this chapter, in all the metros where the ANC lost power to opposition, divisions within the organisation set parameters for the decline in support. In the City of Tshwane and Nelson Mandela Bay Municipality, the infighting and factional tensions within the organisation led to an environment that was not conducive for effective campaigning. In Metsimaholo Local Municipality, the emergence of the MCA, an organisation that initially enabled the formation of a DA-led coalition, was the direct result of ANC leaders being disconnected from the electorate and membership, and the arrogance that initially characterised the proposed amalgamation with Ngwathe Local Municipality. Johannesburg and Ekurhuleni also experienced their fair share of internal strife – as did all other municipalities where ANC electoral support declined.

But another deeply concerning trend that emerged during this period was the tendency of ANC members to unite with opposition forces in voting out deployed Mayors from Councils. In July 2018, members of the ANC in the Sol Plaatjie Municipality in Kimberly, Northern Cape Province, voted with the DA to remove the Mayor through a motion of no confidence. In February 2020, the Executive Mayor and Speaker of the Lekwa Local Municipality in the Gert Sibande District Municipality in Standerton, Mpumalanga Province, were ousted through a motion of no confidence that had been brought on by the DA. This was despite the DA having only five seats to the ANC's 23 in the 30-person Council. Most of those who had voted the Executive Mayor and Speaker out were members of the ANC. According to Viljoen (2020), the two were responsible for the calamitous financial situation that the municipality found itself in. In the same year, Olly Mlamleni, the Mayor of the Mangaung Metropolitan Municipality in the Free State Province, was removed through a motion of no confidence that was brought by the Freedom Front Plus. Mlamleli had been elected in 2016, but her administration had been dogged by allegations of financial mismanagement, poor governance and corruption. She had survived two prior motions. And just this February, the Mayor of Maqwassi Hills Local Municipality in Wolmaranstad in the North West Province was removed through a motion of no confidence brought by F4SD and supported by at least thirteen ANC Councillors.

The simplistic way of looking at this tendency would be to conclude that members of the ANC who are voting with opposition parties to remove leaders deployed by the organisation are ill-disciplined and must be punished. This punitive approach has significant limitations. For one thing, such members are not unaware of the fate that awaits them when they choose to disregard the party line so brazenly. They know too well that they will be subjected to disciplinary action and most certainly removed from their positions. And yet, they take this risk, which affects their livelihoods, to make a political statement. It is perhaps necessary that as an organisation, we reflect deeply on whether this tendency is the result of our own refusal to hold accountable political deployees who underperform in municipalities. It is not an accident of history that, rightly or not, those who have been removed through assisted motions of no confidence were accused of failing on issues related to service delivery, maladministration, and corruption. Whether the allegations are true or not, the ANC learned the hard way how the perception formed by voters and shaped by the organisation's own actions can have a devastating impact on the party's electoral fortunes. The assumption that the ANC is an uncaring organisation alienated the youth from the organisation in 2016. It also made the party lose Metsimaholo Local Municipality and other municipalities. As part of engaging in self-introspection, the issue of ANC members voting out their own deployees must be analysed in its layeredness. The organisation can ill-afford further divisions.

4

THE COALITION GOVERNMENT IN THE CITY OF EKURHULENI

Election Results

The coalition government in the City of Ekurhuleni came into existence following the 2016 local government elections. As was the case with all the metros in the Gauteng Province, the ANC was unable to receive a majority, although it maintained plurality. In these elections, the ANC obtained 49.04 percent of the total vote against the DA's 34.43 percent (Independent Electoral Commission, 2016). The EFF won 25 seats in Council, comprised of one ward seat and twenty-four proportional representation (PR) seats. The AIC won four PR seats while the IFP and Freedom Front Plus gained two each. The Pan Africanist Congress of Azania (PAC), the Patriotic Alliance (PA), the Congress of the People (COPE) and the Independent Ratepayers Association of South Africa (IRASA) each won one PR seat. Because there was no outright winner, this resulted in a hung Council that necessitated the formation of a coalition in the country's fourth biggest metropolitan municipality. An ANC-led coalition was thus formally formed with the AIC, PAC, PA and IRASA. The IFP entered into an agreement to partner with the coalition on key issues, although this was not formalised within the constructs of the formal coalition.

The History of Ekurhuleni and Conditions that Led to the ANC's Decline in Support

The 2016 local government election was the first time in the City of Ekurhuleni's establishment as a metropolitan municipality that the ANC had lost power in the region. Although this was the case with all the metros lost by the organisation across the country, the case of Ekurhuleni is especially nuanced given the history of struggle in the communities – tied closely to the ANC and the broader mass democratic movement. Ekurhuleni, also referred to as the East Rand, was the site of intense political violence between the ANC and IFP in the latter years of apartheid. Townships in the region, particularly Thokoza and Katlehong, were greatly traumatised by this violent conflict that resulted in the deaths of hundreds of people. These were not only those belonging to rival political parties but ordinary people whose only crime was to live in "territories" marked as ANC or IFP. Kynoch (2013) provides a nuanced perspective on this political violence, arguing that while the IFP was responsible for much of the violence, aided by police and military groups, ANC-affiliated militants also conducted murderous campaigns. And while on the ANC's part the violence was largely retaliatory, the political environment of the East Rand had always been highly charged. Support for the ANC in this part of the country was thus grounded in a history of struggle. It was embedded in the hearts of families and communities that had lived through the IFP instigated and apartheid-state sanctioned brutality that characterised the late 1980s and early 1990s.

However, by 2016, there was a sense of dejection with the trajectory of the democratic project, which many believe is employing a glacial pace in the transformation of society. To understand this sentiment necessitates understanding the socio-economic and spatial conditions of Ekurhuleni, which are still reflective of the amoral past.

The City of Ekurhuleni metropolitan municipality was established only twenty-one years ago in 2000, superseding the Eastern Gauteng Services Council, the Khayalami Metropolitan Council, and the previous administrations of Alberton, Benoni, Boksburg, Brakpan, Edenvale/Lethabong, Germiston, Kempton Park/Tembisa, Nigel and Springs (City of Ekurhuleni, 2020). The establishment of this municipality was the logical conclusion to a protracted struggle by the democratic government of South Africa to annihilate the vestiges of our apartheid past – a past that continues to find expression in our spatiality. In merging these historically fragmented locales into one municipality, the democratic government succeeded in undermining the legacy of separate development that had made it improbable to bring about meaningful material change in the lives of the oppressed majority who to this day continue to navigate the difficulties informed by that legacy.

It is important, therefore, to understand that the Ekurhuleni municipality that was inherited by the first-ever Mayor, the late Ambassador Bavumile Vilakazi, is not the same metropolitan municipality that we live in today. Spatially, the municipality was severely underdeveloped in areas that were historically demarcated for Black and Coloured people. As was the case everywhere in the country, the apartheid regime had succeeded in ensuring that these areas were infrastructurally underdeveloped. The result of this underdevelopment led to lack of access to meaningful opportunities in education, healthcare, and other public services. Prior to the establishment of the metro, there was extraordinarily little institutional assistance provided to the residents of Ekurhuleni, particularly in townships and outside historically White suburbs. It was only in 2004 that Customer Care Centres were established to assist residents of the City with municipal services. These had only been accessible to historically White areas. The bucket system was also prominent in Black townships. The bucket system, which refers to a basic form of a dry toilet whereby a bucket (pail) is used to collect excreta, was one of the more dehumanising systems that the apartheid regime subjected Black people to. The system was developed due to the apartheid government's deliberate underdevelopment of townships and rural areas, and denial of water and sanitation infrastructure to Black people. It was an intentional denial of sanitation services that was meant to cement the idea of Black people as unhygienic and diseased. Deprivation was also evident in the roads and transport system. In 2000, there was a backlog of more than 1 500 km of untarred roads (City of Ekurhuleni, 2020), which hampered mobility in historically disadvantaged areas that were predominantly Black. A significant proportion of residents also had no access to electricity. It is for this reason that in the 2002/2003 financial year, ninety percent of the electricity budget was spent on the electrification of previously disadvantaged areas (City of Ekurhuleni, 2020). Free 50 KW of electricity and 6 KL of water per household were provided to all poor residents of the City – nearly all of whom were Black or Coloured.

It is thus no accident of history that even today, while the City of Ekurhuleni is the youngest metro in the Gauteng Province, it has a more pronounced spatial legacy of apartheid. There are over a hundred and twenty informal settlements in the metro. In addition to this, the City of Ekurhuleni has five (or twenty-five percent) of the top twenty biggest townships in South Africa (Statistics SA, 2016). These are Tembisa, Katlehong, Vosloorus, Etwatwa and Tsakane. The demographic tension that binds race, class, and gender – in the context of stubborn and diabolical apartheid spatial planning – is dramatically defined in the City. And while there have been significant inroads made in dealing with these historical challenges and to give dignity to people historically deprived of it, the more salient of these problems persist. It is this that has rendered some of our people somewhat dejected and increasingly feeling that there is inadequate political will to radically transform their material conditions. This played a role in the election outcomes of 2016 – as did the political tensions within the ANC.

Towards the said local government elections, there was some tension and disunity within the organisation, making it difficult to present the needed united front in the campaigning. At the centre of this was opposition to the proposed Mayoral candidate (myself). This view, although held by a small faction within the organisation, created tensions that saw attempts at de-campaigning me. As a democrat at heart, it has always been my contention that political difference is necessary for growth and reflection. But the events of 2016 were not rooted in genuine political difference and, importantly, they undermined the capacity of the ANC to mobilise and campaign effectively. In this sense, difference was costly to the future of the organisation – distinguishing it from the kind of difference and dissent I support that is aimed at strengthening the debates and changing the thinking of the party towards the progressive. The previous chapter demonstrates that the ANC's loss of power in the metros following the 2016 local government elections was the result of not only the economic and socio-political factors prevailing at the time, but the result of fractures within the organisation. Where the

ANC was not united, it was significantly weakened and therefore removed from office. But where there was unity, even in the face of economic and socio-political challenges, there was electoral victory even as the comparative percentage of support declined. This is true of municipalities across the country, including metropolitan municipalities that the organisation retained, namely, the City of eThekwini, the Mangaung Metropolitan Municipality and Buffalo City Metropolitan Municipality. This communicates an important message about organisational unity as a central pillar for organisational survival.

Motions of No Confidence

The City of Ekurhuleni has been lauded as the most stable coalition government to have emerged from the 2016 local government elections. Indeed, ours has been a coalition that has stood the test of time, with the administration completing its full term of office. But while we pride ourselves on this reality, we also acknowledge that there have undoubtedly been significant problems within the coalition itself and the government of the City. For one thing, the DA tabled two motions of no confidence against me. Both motions, supported by opposition parties including the EFF, were largely based on allegations of poor service delivery and my alleged failure to deal with corruption within the metro. In the first motion, the DA alleged maladministration in the City's challenges with diesel supply as well as the deactivation of the C-track system that was installed in Ekurhuleni emergency vehicles. The latter, a result of delayed payment by the City, which was timeously resolved, was a challenge inherited from the previous administration. The DA, however, sought to present it as a direct result of our administration's disregard for the people of the metro.

In the second motion of no confidence, issues of service delivery were also at the centre. In addition to this, the DA also argued that I had misled Council and the citizens of Ekurhuleni when I indicated that the Head of Department for Environment and Waste Management had been suspended. Another point that was raised in the motion related to the Armoury Report that had not at the time been served in Council. Despite the opposition vote, the motion failed. Importantly, the motion that was supposedly in the best interests of Ekurhuleni citizens was rejected by these same persons, who came from across various townships and suburbs to demonstrate support towards the sitting administration on the day of the motion. This show of support was a clear proclamation that multitudes of Ekurhuleni residents did not, in fact, hold the view that they were being deprived of services.

But another factor of great importance is that in both motions of no confidence, the alliance stood steadfast in its support of my leadership and made this fact known to the public. There was never any doubt in the minds of our coalition partners that the DA was engaged in destructive politics that sought to deliberately destabilise the metro, perhaps with the hope of forcing the coalition into a state of instability as was happening with other municipalities across the country. Throughout our term of office, opposition has sustained its onslaught on the coalition not only through motions of no confidence but also through a disregard and distortion of the important work that the coalition is doing in the City. However, the quality of the work that we have done in the last five years, including work done in the 2020-2021 period that was defined by the devastating COVID-19 global pandemic, has consistently spoken for itself against the false narratives that the DA has sought to peddle. Later in this chapter, some of these major achievements, including assessments made by independent institutions, will be analysed.

The Coalition Experience in the City of Ekurhuleni

As explained, the coalition government in the City of Ekurhuleni was not without its own share of challenges. But unlike other metros and municipalities that collapsed, the challenges that were faced by the Ekurhuleni coalition were the result of the opposition's discontent as demonstrated in the motions of no confidence, rather than in fractures within the formal coalition itself. This, however, does not imply that there were no disagreements within the coalition. In this section, I will detail the experiences of all coalition partners. These highlight the strengths, weaknesses, opportunities, and threats that were observed by different parties who constituted the coalition government.

The Interview Processes

Unlike the interviews in the City of Tshwane, the City of Johannesburg and elsewhere, in which I actively participated in interviewing the participants, interviews of coalition partners in the City of Ekurhuleni were done exclusively by the lead researcher for this book. I participated in the first interview with the coalition partners only because this was introductory and aimed at providing a background of the project undertaken. However, I was not part of subsequent interviews. The reason for this was two-fold. Firstly, coalition partners were interviewed in their capacity as representatives of political organisations. Secondly, to ensure that the partners spoke of their own volition, it was necessary to allow them the independence to engage an objective interviewer who, unlike me, is not a direct participant in the coalition arrangement. Such an approach makes allowance for open and honest discussion, adding to the credibility of the data collected.

Interviews with the City of Ekurhuleni coalition partners were conducted virtually, with follow-ups done telephonically. As with other interviews, the interview was semi-structured, combining the unstructured interview and a structured interview to the gain advantages of both. While some set questions were posed, the interviewees could express their opinions and ask the interviewer questions during the interview, which encouraged them to give more useful information such as their opinions toward sensitive issues. The same questions posed in the interviews in Chapter three were used. The following is a comprehensive summary of the interviews from all coalition partners. It must be noted that while the IFP was not in a formal coalition with the ANC in Ekurhuleni, but did have an arrangement of cooperation, it was also interviewed as part of the coalition.

Coalition Partner One

Coalition Partner One argued that the ANC's loss of electoral support in the 2016 local government elections was the result of broader societal issues that the organisation was confronted with provincially and nationally. Central to this was the issue of e-tolls in the Gauteng Province, which many motorists were opposed to but which at the time, the ANC-led government was insisting on imposing without having done due public consultation. The Councillor argued that e-tolls were an arrogant demonstration of power on the part of the governing party which did not deem it necessary to engage the public in dialogue before forcefully implementing the service. Already paying exorbitant income taxes and having many other financial responsibilities, voters were of the view that the ANC as an organisation was not committed to easing financial burdens on them and this thinking was taken to the polling stations. In addition to this, the 2016 local government elections took place at a time when the ANC's public image had been battered by several scandals. This, the Councillor argued, influenced voters at a local level, and combined with slow service delivery, informed the voting patterns of 2016.

In terms of the formation of the coalition, the Councillor argued that his organisation had to think deeply about who to support, the DA or the ANC, but ultimately settled on the ANC because it had obtained most of the votes and needed only a few coalition partners to govern. The DA, he argued, had obtained 32 percent of the vote, and would have needed more coalition partners. The Councillor argued that his party was worried that there would be no stability if a party that obtained only 32 percent of the vote governed. Additionally, his party did not trust the EFF. For this coalition partner, stability was instrumental in being part of the coalition. A hung or conflict-ridden Council would not be able to approve budgets, which would result in disruptions to service delivery for residents of the City. And so, when approached by the ANC to form part of the coalition, the party readily agreed. The Councillor's constituency as well as the DA strongly disapproved of this decision and he was subjected to colossal verbal abuse. As a result, for the first eight months, his party had to call meetings to explain the decision to the community. This was made easy by the collective distrust of the EFF which in other coalitions across the country was proving to be problematic.

The Councillor indicated that there were some disagreements in the coalition as well as a difference of opinion in terms of the allocation of portfolios. He had wanted a particular portfolio, but the ANC would not agree to it, thus resulting in a compromise to a different portfolio. Differences also expressed themselves in Council where on two or three occasions, his party voted against the ANC. However, this did not in any way destabilise the coalition. The Councillor indicated that he had been deeply committed to the stability of the coalition and as a result, did not support motions of no confidence against the Executive Mayor.

The Councillor indicated that the coalition government did more for his community than he had been able to do for fifteen years as a Councillor. He attributed this to the fact that as a partner in the coalition, his opinions mattered more and were taken into consideration, thus bringing about meaningful change to the lives of community members who in the end realised the effectiveness of the coalition. His party contends that the most important component in making a coalition work is effective and constant communication. The coalition in the City of Ekurhuleni survived because there was good communication, and the party believes that coalition governments are the future of South African politics. But to make these stable, the party argues that the party with the most votes within the coalition must field Members of the Mayoral Committee in order that there is no breakage with the party's electoral commitments that could be compromised by an unstable Mayoral committee.

Coalition Partner Two

Coalition Partner Two indicated that the ANC's loss of electoral support in the City of Ekurhuleni was largely the result of the ANC-led government's lack of commitment to service delivery issues over a long period of time, in Ekurhuleni and across the country. He contended that the last two decades of democracy had been characterised by significant failures on the part of the governing party, and that while initially the people of South Africa were willing to chalk this up to the monumental feat of redressing injustices of an apartheid system that had been deeply embedded in the fibre of the very make-up of the South African society, it had gotten to a point where people were no longer willing to be patient or understanding of the reported maladministration, misappropriation of state resources and rampant corruption that had come to define the party. Another issue of concern to the voter, according to the interviewee, was the party's arrogance in the electoral campaign. The ANC's electoral slogan for the 2016 local government elections had been "Asinavalo", which directly translates to "We have no fear". This slogan, which the organisation had used to communicate its gallant and fearless spirit in the face of difficulty, was interpreted by many people as being an act of defiance and lack of remorse, particularly due to the political climate prevailing at the time, with the ANC President Jacob Zuma being a subject of controversy due to the Nkandla imbroglio, which the ANC NEC defended, and which ANC members of parliament initially defended even after the Public Protector had raised important questions around the use of taxpayers' money in what she argued was for personal benefit by the former president. This show of arrogance, according to coalition Partner Two, was indicative of an organisation that was tone deaf to the plight of the poor and the views of the people whom it had long since begun to treat as nothing more than voting fodder.

According to the Councillor, his party was not initially keen on entering a coalition with the ANC in the City of Ekurhuleni. This was due in great part to the political tensions between his organisation and the ANC at a national level. The national leaders of the two parties did not see eye-to-eye on many political issues and this had a great impact on the engagements at local government level. When his party ultimately went into a coalition with the ANC in the said metro, it was mainly because the national committee understood that the two parties, while having vastly different political objectives, were fundamentally representatives of the same constituency. Therefore, it was necessary that they put their differences aside to ensure that communities are served.

Coalition Partner Two was extremely critical of the coalition government, arguing that the arrogance that had influenced the ANC's loss of power in the City and across the country was manifested in how the organisation related to other parties within the coalition. He contended that the ANC-led coalition did not accord its coalition partners the recognition they deserved, and that there was inadequate communication about critical matters that the coalition should have been engaged in. In addition to this, it was the opinion of the Councillor that there was inadequate service delivery in hostels and informal settlements where his party's constituency was mainly located. This created a sense of disillusionment in these communities around the effectiveness of the coalition.

Coalition Partner Two has served as a councillor since 1995 and indicated that he had gone on study tours to different countries to understand how governments, including coalition governments, function. He contends that for a coalition government to function effectively, there needs to be constant proactive communication and not reactive communication that happens only in response to challenges. And while he believes that coalition governments are the future of South African politics, he argues that they need to be managed better to ensure that they work for the benefit of voters. Asked whether he could consider working within an ANC-led coalition government again, the Councillor stated that it was something about which he was unsure.

Coalition Partner Three

Coalition Partner Three argued that the ANC's loss of electoral support in the City of Ekurhuleni was the result of its lack of prioritisation of Coloured communities who have been on the receiving end of neglect by the state. The Councillor argued that Coloured areas were neglected by the ANC in the City of Ekurhuleni whose focus was on providing services to informal settlements that are predominantly Black and not so much backyard dwellings where working-class Coloured people mainly reside. This issue of human settlements played a huge role in the sense of dejection that was being experienced in the Coloured communities where the neglect extended to lack of communication with them on the part of the local state. The Councillor argued that identity politics in South Africa are strengthening, evidenced in the growth of conservative White nationalist parties such as the Freedom Front Plus as well as the exponential growth of the EFF, which is committed to the empowerment and liberation of Black people. In the Northern Cape Province, he contended, the Coloured community identified more with the first nation movements, hence the strong emergence of Khoisan political activists.

The Councillor argued that the ANC that was once a beacon of hope for the Coloured community, which was instrumental in the United Democratic Front support of the ideals of the ANC, had neglected it – a fact echoed by the Gauteng Premier David Makhura. Speaking at the opening of the ANC's provincial conference in Irene in 2018, Makhura posited: "I have come across indisputable evidence of serious neglect by our government and under-investment in the coloured communities of our province. This neglect has far-reaching consequences... Crime and drugs have increased while the standard of living has dropped including a decline in educational achievement and advancement among our people in these communities. Both poverty and unemployment have reached extreme levels. This has bred resentment and anger" (Umraw, 2018). But according to the Councillor, the ANC government's neglect of the Coloured community is evident in what he deems is tribalism within the organisation, which has seen a number of Coloured supporters like himself move away from the organisation.

In terms of the formation of the coalition, the party was approached by the ANC to be part of the coalition and agreed. The party was unwilling to work with the DA, which it regards as an exceptionally racist party that has no interest in the development and empowerment of any communities that are not White. It also held the view that within a coalition, it was best positioned to hold the ANC-led government accountable. As with Coalition Partner One, this interviewee indicated that his constituency was displeased with the decision to enter a coalition with the ANC and that his party needed to engage in a process of educating the voters about what a coalition means and what it could accomplish.

The Councillor stated that the coalition government in the City of Ekurhuleni had not always been stable and that earlier on in the arrangement his party had almost pulled out of it. This was due to a lack of communication on the part of the ANC as the leader of the coalition, which gave his party the sense that the ANC wanted to govern as though outside a coalition arrangement. The Councillor also raised a concern about the arrogance of the administrative staff of the municipality, particularly from those aligned to the ANC. He contended that the Heads of Departments and Divisional Heads who were members of the ANC demonstrated partisan allegiance in how they engaged coalition partners, and that this could have potentially devastated the coalition government. He insisted, however, that the Executive Mayor was the glue that held it all together due to his own character of fairness and being approachable. The party to which Coalition Partner Two belonged had wanted a portfolio based on the priority of their constituency and was able to chair the portfolio where significant work was being done in the municipality.

The Councillor contended that ordinary people no longer want one party to govern as this deepens corruption. This is the case not only in South Africa but across the African continent where former national liberation movements are increasingly being dislodged from power by emerging political parties that are more open to the coalition arrangement, as is the case in Egypt and elsewhere on the continent. Coalitions, he argued, are the future of politics in South Africa. But to be strengthened and stabilised, it is necessary that communication is prioritised by coalition partners. He further indicated that smaller parties in coalitions must be firm on what they want and must demand to chair critical portfolios as well as be part of Mayoral committees. Making an example of the City of Johannesburg where the current Executive Mayor has been accused of micromanaging departments under the leadership of coalition partners, the interviewee argued that parties must enter into a clear agreement on non-interference by the dominant coalition partner, and that such agreements and others must not be reneged on.

Coalition Partner Four

Coalition Partner Four argued that the loss of power by the ANC in the City of Ekurhuleni was the result of a shifting perspective by the younger generation on the value of former national liberation movements. The democratic dispensation was increasingly becoming neo-liberal and as a result, political parties steeped in resistance and struggle history were being rendered irrelevant by an emergence of a different kind of politics. In addition to this, there was also widespread dejection about the trajectory that the ANC-led government was taking. Service delivery issues were at the core of the discontent that was registered by voters going towards the 2016 local government elections.

In terms of the formation of the coalition, the Councillor indicated that her party agreed to enter a coalition with the ANC largely because it did not want to see the disappearance of former national liberation movements cum governing parties in the Gauteng Province, which is the hub of the South African economy. The two other metros in the province – the City of Johannesburg and the City of Tshwane – had been lost by the ANC to a coalition led by the DA and this worried the interviewee's party as it meant that liberation movements were being dislocated. To the interviewee, former national liberation movements have a historical and moral obligation towards the marginalised and disenfranchised African majority. For this reason, it is necessary that they govern metropolitan municipalities with big budgets that can significantly alter the living conditions of poor Black communities in the country.

The Councillor stated that the main problem that her party faced in the City of Ekurhuleni coalition government was inadequate communication. This, however, was significantly resolved through the establishment of coalition summits and monthly engagements that were aimed at reporting to coalition partners on progress being done and other matters pertaining to the coalition.

While the Councillor believes that coalitions are an inevitable feature of South Africa's future politics, she argued that coalition governments must be premised on important principles rather than convenience. Clear aims and objectives must be determined, as too must clear programmes aimed at bettering the lives of communities. She stated that the interests of the parties entering the coalition must be agreed upon upfront so that there are no hidden agendas that could potentially derail the functioning and stability of the coalition government. The Councillor concluded with a recommendation that parties must establish a clear policy on how to constitute and manage coalitions.

Coalition Partner Five

Coalition Partner Five did not delve into an assessment of what had led to the ANC's loss of electoral support in the City of Ekurhuleni but indicated that the voting patterns across the country were a demonstration of the growing view of South African voters that no one party should be given the mandate to govern. He contended that in terms of the coalition in the City of Ekurhuleni, his party decided to be part because it did not want the Council to be hung, which would have resulted in instability in the municipality. The party did not want a by-election as this would have resulted in additional resources being utilised by the state, which ought to have been directed towards service delivery and bettering the lives of millions of people in the metro. The Councillor stated that the coalition arrangement was not necessarily easy because some compromises had to be made which subordinated the political aspirations of his party. This, however, did not negate the party's desire to see a functional government in the City of Ekurhuleni.

The Councillor stated that the coalition government achieved a great deal for the people of Ekurhuleni, particularly the youth. According to him, the City invested significantly in bursary and scholarship schemes for young people in the metro, ensuring that they are afforded the opportunity to better their lives and the lives of their communities. The Councillor posited that the ANC-led administration's commitment to education and skills development of the youth was a major reason for his party's continued participation in the coalition as this was a common political objective of the ANC and his party, which has unwavering bias towards youth development.

The Councillor believes strongly in the future of coalition governments in South Africa and argues that the most important ingredient to the success of coalitions is teamwork. Communication is also central to a functional coalition government.

Reflections by the Executive Mayor

The ANC, having won 49 percent of the votes in the 2016 local government elections, was compelled to establish a coalition government that would ensure that it would continue to deliver on its electoral mandate to the citizens of the City of Ekurhuleni. Arguments have been posed in this book and elsewhere that the ANC's loss of power was the result of a multitude of factors that converged at a particular political moment. My interpretation is that while this is true, it is also true that politics are evolving. To analyse the electoral outcomes of 2016 as merely a consequence of voters punishing the ANC for service delivery and other issues is simplistic, for it does not factor in the shifting voting patterns of prior and subsequent elections. Evidence before us suggests that long before the Nkandla imbroglio, the emergence of the #FeesMustFall movement and other developments that certainly did contribute to the party's electoral performance, the political ground for the ANC had begun to shift. A new type of voter was already determining the fate of South Africa. This voter is young and while appreciative of the historical constructs from whence the country emerged, is not married to the idea of national liberation movements for their own sake. Curiously, it is the ANC-led government that gave birth to this voter – something about which the organisation must be extremely proud. The conscious, young Black voter who is demanding more from government is the product of education and freedoms which the ANC-led government has provided and fought hard to defend.

The lead researcher of this book is a 29-year-old Black woman who was born and raised in a township in the Gauteng Province, to a poor family that has remained ANC since the days of apartheid. Her family, like millions of others, was removed from an informal settlement into an RDP settlement where they have since built a decent family home. She attended primary school in Soweto but went on to study at former model-C schools that had been integrated by the ANC-led government at the dawn of the democratic dispensation. She proceeded to a prestigious historically White university where even as there were challenges, she was able to access the best public education. Her Honours degree tuition was paid for by the Gauteng Provincial Government after her stellar undergraduate performance, and having obtained the Honours degree cum laude, her Master's degree was partly funded by the ANC-led South African government through resources allocated to public universities to provide financial support in the form of merit bursaries to students who obtain exceptional results. Upon graduation, she was employed at national government. This young woman whose geo-history and life is intertwined with the ANC and its own history is critical of the organisation. When she first became eligible to vote, she did not vote for the ANC even as that would later change upon realisation on her part that it was important to contribute to change in the organisation.

It would be narrow to look at this story and conclude that the youth is ungrateful. For one thing, the mandate of our government is to serve all people regardless of their political allegiances. This is what separates the ANC-led government from those who have failed to distinguish between the party as an autonomous political instrument and as a government. The more useful analysis is one that says that the ANC is doing well in contributing to producing these educated young people who have, because of our policies, emerged from the suffocating throes of poverty and disenfranchisement. Additionally, the fact that the ANC-led government employs and supports these young people who hold dissenting views is evidence of the maturity of our democracy and the organisation's capacity to appreciate difference – something which has always been embedded in the DNA of the organisation. Importantly, these young people who are changing the face of South African politics are not to be rejected or feared, but to be understood and embraced. This is something that the ANC is consistently doing, and a lesson it took from the student protests of 2015-2017. The youth should not be scolded for criticising the ANC – it should be engaged. This is happening in Ekurhuleni and across the country. Such a deep sense of reflection can only come from an organisation that is committed to change and to making South Africa better.

The coalition experience was enlightening for the ANC in the City of Ekurhuleni. Having never had a coalition government before, the City found itself having to manage govern-ance beyond what it was accustomed to and include the coalition partnership as one of its priorities of governing. The argument by coalition partners that communication was initially shaky in the beginning is true. The coalition experience was new for everyone and none of us had a blueprint on how to do it effectively, which is at the heart of why this book is necessary in the discourse on the present and future realities of coalition governments. We learned through experience what it means to govern in a coalition and some mistakes were made, including failure to communicate effectively in the beginning. But we have consistently sought to discover and resolve our weaknesses, and to identify threats and turn them into opportunities for growth and better partner-ship with our coalition partners. It was for this reason that in 2019, the ANC hosted the Local Government Summit aimed at, among other things, finding ways to better manage coalitions in the metros. A presentation by the ANC in Ekurhuleni provided important recommendations that will be summarised in the final chapter.

Key Achievements of the Coalition Government in the City of Ekurhuleni

This year marks the end of the five-year term that was served by the ANC-led coalition in the City of Ekurhuleni. This is the only metropolitan municipality in the Gauteng Province that has maintained the same political leadership from 2016 to 2021. This alone is an indication of the strength of the coalition and its capacity to manage differences in a way that does not impede the stability of the municipality and the delivery of services to the people. Over the past five years, there have been important material and moral victories that the ANC-led coalition government in the City has scored. In this section, I will analyse just six of these that in my opinion have made the greatest difference in the lives of our people. They are: education, coalition governance, service delivery to informal settle-ments, land reform, development of the township economy and the support for Small, Medium and Micro Enterprises (SMMEs), infrastructure development and governance.

Governance

We were clear as a coalition government from the outset that our only chance at success would be to put in place a solid management team in the administration to carry out the operational work required. The key objective here was to build an efficient, clean, accountable, and innovative administration that works firmly within the guidelines of legislation. This is in line with the short-term objectives of the Growth and Development Strategy (2055) which enjoins us to build a City that is managed, efficiently resourced and financially sustainable with no service delivery challenges. This required that we professionalise and align our governance structures, recruit qualified and energetic personnel and senior management, and fill up as many vacancies as necessary. All vacancies in our City were filled in compliance with Employment Equity.

Additionally, the City rolled out the Recognition of Prior Learning (RPL) system to evalu-ate, align and accredit skills acquired over a long period of service within the institution. This was done to ensure that the City's human resources is adequately equipped with the necessary skills to maximise service delivery capacity. The biggest beneficiaries of this ongoing programme are low-skilled employees in the City, who are being capaci-tated with relevant skills to contribute substantively to a modern public service. The City also developed a Knowledge Management Strategy and Policy that was approved by Council. Additionally, we institutionalised a set of policies intended to regulate and underpin our governance operations, all of which were approved by Council. Among these is the Integrity Management Framework.

We introduced a stage gate tracking for planning and Capital Expenditure (Capex) War Room to assess Capex. We also stablished systems to reclaim a Clean Audit and to ensure that previous Auditor General findings are cleared. This was done through quarterly management meetings championed by Internal Audit. Because of these interventions, we have maintained clean and unqualified audits over the past five years, with no unauthorised, irregular, and fruitless expenditure, and a clean audit on performance information. This is a testament of our commitment to good governance and sound financial management. The systems of Governance Risk and Compliance of the City are also stable and effective.

Coalition governance

The City of Ekurhuleni managed to remain a stable coalition government that centres service delivery at its heart. Our capacity to weather storms is grounded on the strength of our governance and the existence of strong and credible institutions that have been built over time in the City. Political management meetings, Mayoral committees, and Caucus and Council meetings are held regularly. The state of the coalition is in good health in as far as governance and party-to-party relations are concerned. A total of twenty-nine monthly coalition meetings were convened between January 2017 and October 2020. The purpose of these was to deliberate on pertinent issues related to governance. At least four successful coalition summits have been held to assess the implementation of the coalition agreements and issues of common interest. The importance of this must not be underestimated. It is precisely because we prioritise these processes that ours is undoubtedly the most stable coalition government among all metros.

Education
The City of Ekurhuleni's incumbent administration was absolutely committed to youth development and empowerment. Our coalition has always been focused on implementing human capital development interventions on behalf of community members. The provision of financial assistance is one of the many initiatives that the City is implementing to achieve its goal of increasing the skills base of the region. In advancing our skills development project, we increased our education allocation to R100 million community bursary fund. This is a 10-fold increase from the previous years when the bursary fund was at R10 million. The net effect of this investment has been an increase in the number of beneficiaries. Over the past four years, we have allocated R400 million to bursaries, to sustain just over eight thousand bursary students in the system at any given time. Of the R100 million per annum bursary investment, R5 million is invested towards an international scholarship programme with numerous students who are receiving their education at Breda University in the Netherlands. Some of these students have graduated and are already ploughing back into the country.

When we assumed office in 2016, we committed that we would relentlessly pursue the issue of the establishment of a university in the City of Ekurhuleni. We made this commitment understanding the Herculean task that it would be to lobby all relevant stakeholders and knowing full well the extraordinarily huge responsibility that we would be placing on our shoulders. This goal finally materialised when the President of the Republic of South Africa, His Excellency Cyril Ramaphosa, announced in his 2020 State of the Nation Address that the Ekurhuleni University of Innovation, Science and Technology would be established. Developments are now underway to ensure that the university is built. This is a giant leap that will ensure that our City becomes an intellectual hub for scientists, innovators, and technologists who are much needed in our economy.

Service delivery in informal settlements
In commencing with our term of office in 2016, we outlined a vivid programme of action to advance a pro-poor agenda where the driving force is a people-centred governance. We defined this agenda as a deliberate and systematic bias to rollout service delivery and economic development opportunities in a manner that uplifts the poorest sections of Ekurhuleni, in line with the pro-poor philosophy of administrations before us. The

coalition government in our City was effective precisely because there was a general agreement on who needed to be prioritised: the poor and most marginalised communities in informal settlements.

Service delivery improved significantly in the City under our administration, particularly in informal settlements where we invested a great deal of resources in electrification and creating a habitable environment. We rolled out an informal settlement electrification programme that led to the installation of 33 236 photovoltaic lighting panels in the last financial year. So far, the City has electrified 8 981 households in informal settlements. This brings the total number of connected households in informal settlements to 22 516. Waste and sanitation services were also prioritised. As part of the integration of informal settlements, our administration reduced the household ratio of chemical toilets from 1:10 to 1:5. This means that whereas before ten families in informal settlements shared one toilet, we were able to reduce this by exactly half. This was done because our coalition was united on the position that the poorest sections of our City needed to be humanised. Our work with historically disenfranchised communities also extended to townships. The City accomplished its target of township regularisation of thirty-nine townships. The thirty-nine townships will yield 32 559 title deeds to be distributed to the beneficiaries. It is important that we understand that title deeds are not only legal documents used as evidence of home ownership – they are a source of security for people who for many decades have lived in a state of insecurity.

The success of our pro-poor philosophy of governance and service delivery was confirmed by the results of the 5th Gauteng City-Region Observatory Quality of Life Survey. According to this survey, overall, we are doing better than almost all municipalities in Gauteng. More instructive is the fact that we are a leader of our peer-group of metros. We performed better than all the other metros in terms of the level of citizen satisfaction in the Quality-of-Life assessment. The City was ranked as the city affording its citizens with the highest quality of life in comparison to other metros in the province. Specifically, we were certified as having outperformed the other metros in the areas of delivering water services, renewable energy, and sanitation services. Our performance in healthcare has also been exemplary. The City achieved position one in the Gauteng Province and overall position number two in the country on the Ideal Clinic Realisation and Maintenance – an initiative in preparation for the National Health Insurance.

Infrastructure development
When we commenced with our term of office in 2016, we embarked on a process of building twenty-nine reservoirs. Thus far, water storages with a combined 55 megalitres have been completed. Other water storages are underway. When complete, this infrastructure will add an additional 417 megalitres of storage to the existing 954 megalitres. This will translate to approximately an additional 12 hours additional storage bringing the City's storage capacity to 36 hrs.

Additionally, in the first year of our term, the City acquired land for housing opportunities to be rolled out through six Mega Human Settlements Projects. These include the Tembisa Ext 25 Mega Project that will yield a total of 3 510 housing units. Of these, 3 159 are RDP walk-ups and the remaining 351 are Social Housing Units that are being built as four storey walk-ups. The City is currently in the process of constructing three other Mega Projects, namely, John Dube, Daggafontein and Leeuwpoort with a combined total yield of 50 571 units. We are also building more units in various areas, namely, Clayville, Chief Albert Luthuli Ext 6 and Tsakane Ext 22. The combined delivered RDP units is 4 754 while 5 647 serviced stands have been provided. The combined total yield of these is 27 154. Another achievement that is important to note is that through our Social Labour Plan, we developed a partnership with AfriSam to construct houses for people with disabilities and youth-headed households. Construction of these houses in Mackenzieville has been completed.

Since 2016, two fire stations have been opened in the City of Ekurhuleni. These are the Thokoza Fire Station and Germiston Central Fire Station, opened in 2017 and 2018, respectively. These are only some of the key infrastructure projects that our administration undertook that are aimed at developing the City.

Support for SMMEs and development of the township economy
The coalition government was deeply committed to building an efficient local economy that addresses the material needs of our Small, Medium and Micro Enterprises (SMMEs) and communities. It must be recognised that for greater progress to be achieved, there is a need to create platforms to encourage, explore, support, and provide opportunities for development and growth of small and medium enterprises. In 2019, we officially opened the Kwa-Thema Business Hub. This hub is one of the various facilities that the City is developing in townships. These facilities are aimed at providing office space to small businesses at an affordable rate. The hub provides entrepreneurs with professional meeting space and training facilities. Kwa Thema SMME Business Hub is considered to contribute as a driver of the promotion of local township revitalisation within the City. In addition to this, the facility has contributed to the promotion of the City's Massive Infrastructure Investment Programme, which is key in supporting the growth and development of SMMEs, which will aid development and growth in the region. It is used as an SMME Empowerment Precinct that will house various development funding institutions and SMMEs, including a Catering Support Incubation in partnership with Tiger Brands and SEDA/Gibela Incubation. The facility consists of thirty-two office units and twelve industrial units that will be rented out to SMMEs.

Land reform
Land is a fundamental resource without which the development and growth of all other resources is improbable. This is an understanding that was shared by the ANC-led coalition. For this reason, we have done a great deal of work in ensuring that land is at the

centre of our economic as well as social cohesion efforts. We embarked on speeding up the release of strategic land to facilitate investments in identified sectors, particularly manufacturing and agriculture, in support of the 10-Point Economic Plan of the City. The initiative is linked to the GDS 2055 Imperative on job creation, economic growth, and social empowerment. The process to release land for strategic development was started by our administration with fifty-six farms being released. The primary objective is to boost agricultural growth and job creation. Additionally, there is an ongoing process of identification of thirty properties for Industrial Development that are more than 4 000 square metres, suitably zoned for industrial purposes in townships. A further ninety-nine properties, which are less than 5 000 square metres, suitably zoned for commercial purposes, have been identified in townships.

These are only some of the achievements that were made possible by the ANC-led coalition in the City of Ekurhuleni, and which will outlive our government. Their impact on the lives of our people is enormous and will only be fully understood and qualified in years to come when the metro assumes its rightful place as not just the manufacturing and logistics hub of sub-Saharan Africa, but as an intellectual and economic hub for the region, in the mould of bigger metropolitan municipalities such as the City of Johannesburg.

5

INTERVIEW WITH MZILIKAZI WA AFRIKA

This book is more than an undertaking pertaining to reflections on the realities and future of coalition governments in South Africa. It is also, in many ways, a conversation-starter about the need for re-imagining democracy and therefore, centring important institutions in the process. The media is without doubt one of the most important institutions that form the foundation on which strong democracies are built. It is an agency of socialisation that shapes and influences the thinking of society. For this reason, it is only fitting that a chapter in this book be dedicated to a frank discussion between myself and a journalist who has never shied away from asking uncomfortable questions and above all, speaking truth to power.

Leonard Mzilikazi Ndzukula, known to many as Mzilikazi Wa Afrika, is a seasoned investigative journalist who has worked for various national newspapers including the *Sunday Times* and the *Sunday Independent*. In 2010, when national discourse was centred around the proposed Media Appeals Tribunal and Protection of Information Bill, which drew a lot of condemnation from opposition parties and civil society alike, Wa Afrika was arrested in what was believed to have been politically motivated harassment after he exposed the controversial R500 million property rental deal (Wa Afrika & Hofstatter, 2010). In the explosive article, Wa Afrika had stated that the deal never went out to tender, violating National Treasury regulations that all contracts over R500 000 must go through a competitive bid process. He would go on to expose many other troubling issues in government.

To have Wa Afrika as part of the conversation on the present and future realities of coalition governments in South Africa is not an accident of history, but a deliberate effort at communicating that the work of the media is a fundamental cornerstone of a healthy democracy and a transparent government, and that any government that fashions a higher civilisation must not be afraid of accounting to the media on matters of public interest – no matter how uncomfortable these may be. In ensuring that this book communicates the salient message that it seeks to about coalition government, but that journalistic freedoms are also protected, Wa Afrika was given carte blanche to ask the questions he wanted to ask relating to the subject, as well as some aspects of the political realities of the ANC.

I am genuinely surprised, Executive Mayor, that you chose a journalist who is not popular in some circles of the African National Congress, to do this interview with

A story is told of an ANC member who went to Tanzania following the 1976 student uprisings in South Africa. Upon his arrival there, he sat down with a senior ANC leader and raised his concerns about the growing Black Consciousness Movement that was attracting scores of young Black people, many of whom were rejecting the ANC and other national liberation movements, arguing that these had become redundant after being forced underground. The ANC member, frustrated at what he perceived as militant, anti-ANC youth, asked the senior leader what needed to be done about these young people who, left to their own devices, would displace the ANC in the imagination of the people. After contemplating the question for a few minutes, the senior ANC leader responded: "What needs to be done is that these young people should be brought into the ANC".

Are you saying you are recruiting me into the ANC?

I am saying the ANC has never been afraid of people who hold different opinions – it is what makes it such a strong organisation. Your dissenting views do not negate the fact that you have a reputation as someone who asks the important questions, and this is more important to any intellectual project than personal feelings about a person.

Besides, the ANC is a home for all South Africans – you included.

Like many South Africans, I am extremely interested in understanding what led to the writing of this book

An American astronomer and author, Carl Edward Sagan, reflecting on the necessity to preserve and support libraries, said: "The health of our civilization, the depth of our awareness about the underpinnings of our culture and our concern for the future can all be tested by how well we support our libraries". This profound argument has always shaped my relationship with the ideational space and is at the heart of why I wanted this book to be written.

The 2016 local government election was a particularly important political moment in the life of our country. It shaped the political milieu in a way that little else has done before or since and forced all of us as political activists and government practitioners to re-imagine the world in which we exist. The emergence of coalition governments in the metros forced us to think about a future in which the ANC is not hegemonic, at least electorally. What would this future look like and what would it mean for the people of South Africa? We saw empirical evidence that coalition governments can be messy and destructive – but we also saw some great examples of how they can work. And so, if there is a possibility that coalitions are part of our politics and our future, as is happening across the world, it becomes important that we document our experiences in being part of them and find ways to think about making them better in future so that whatever happens, the people of our country do not bear the brunt of our limitations in governing. What happened in some of our metros, specifically in the City of Tshwane where governance literally came to a standstill due to political conflicts that affected service delivery, should not happen again. To ensure this, we must begin to speak frankly and progressively about how we form coalitions that are stable and effective.

Some would argue that you have been flirting with the opposition, specifically, the EFF. Is there any truth to this, or do you still believe very strongly in the ruling party?

As a starting point, I must be clear that South Africa is a constitutional democracy and the ANC a democratic organisation. By definition, the ANC is not a ruling party but rather, a governing party mandated by an electoral majority to administer affairs of the state. It is important to emphasise this because characterising the ANC as a ruling party implies that it does not have legitimacy to govern and that its will is imposed. This could create a false narrative that seeks to question the legitimacy of the party – something that is already happening in some spaces.

The idea that I am flirting with the EFF is neither new nor true, and is based largely on my personal relationship with EFF leader, Julius Malema, who is a friend and brother to me. There is an insistence in our country of erasing history, of pretending that certain things did not happen. For many years, Malema was a committed member of the ANC and someone with whom many of us built a lasting relationship. That we now sit on opposite political benches does not negate the fact that we have a relationship grounded in mutual respect and shared history. The ANC that I grew up in is not an organisation that is obsessed with policing who its members relate with, provided that such relationships are not an affront to the ideals of the national democratic society that we are building. There is no basis, therefore, for my relationship with Malema or any member of the EFF to not exist, or to be criminalised in the manner that it is. From where I sit, such thinking betrays an infantile approach to politics.

I joined the ANC at a young age because of the vision that it represented for South Africa. Having grown up in an East Rand that was marred by immeasurable violence and structural inequalities, I was drawn to this organisation that sought to fashion a higher civilisation for all South Africans. That ideal has not changed. The ANC remains committed to creating a better life for all and has demonstrated this through its adoption of pro-poor policies that are among some of the most progressive in the world. For this reason, I continue to believe wholeheartedly in the party and its capacity to make South Africa better.

So, neither you nor members of the ANC close to you are considering the formation of a splinter organisation despite some of your public disagreements with what you deem a glacial pace in actualising some of the key resolutions of the 54th National Conference?

Members of the ANC are committed to strengthening the organisation because they understand that the prosperity of South Africa depends on a strong, ethical, and united ANC and the broader mass democratic movement. I do not believe that ANC members are sitting around contemplating the possibility of breaking away from the organisation – I am certainly not. That would indicate that they have decided that the organisation is irredeemable and incapable of carrying out the electoral mandate that it has been given by millions of South Africans, which could not be further from the truth.

History is littered with numerous examples of political parties that have split from the ANC. Pre-democracy, we had members of the ANC breaking away to establish the Pan Africanist Congress of Azania (PAC) and in the democratic dispensation we had breakaways that led to the formation of the United Democratic Movement (UDM), the Congress of the People (COPE) and recently, the Economic Freedom Fighters (EFF). While these organisations have their own ideological and philosophical differences, the common denominator among them is that none have been able to successfully wrestle state power from the ANC. This is in part because many a South African voter, even with the problems that the organisation has, believes in the vision of the ANC. It is something that no breakaway party has successfully managed to annihilate. For this reason, I am not convinced that a breakaway would work – I am convinced that unity, not creating splinter organisations, is the answer.

And yet you have accused ANC Leaders of not implementing conference resolutions

The ANC has always been an organisation that welcomes debate and where different perspectives can exist at the same time. There are certain things that happen in the organisation which I do not agree with, and I will not shy away from raising my views about those things. I believe that the organisation adopted some important resolutions at the Nasrec conference – resolutions which, if implemented, could result in radical economic transformation. I believe that these resolutions must be implemented – particularly the resolutions on the expropriation of land without compensation and the nationalisation of the South African Reserve Bank.

Why must the Reserve Bank be nationalised?

Currently, the primary mandate of the Reserve Bank is to achieve price stability. This is generally interpreted to mean stable and low inflation of between 3 and 6 percent in our case. The monetary policy of South Africa is the exclusive reserve of the Bank. The Reserve Bank should have at least two primary mandates: price stability and growth/employment. What this means is that the Reserve Bank should be given a sustainable employment target over and above the inflation target. This is a global practice done in developed countries as indicated.

Having an employment target will prevent the economy from experiencing prolonged recessions, due to interest rates being high. An employment mandate would moderate the interest rate policy so that it is more sensitive and explicitly so, to the pulse of the real economy. The central bank needs to have both the price and employment target to do that. In addition to this, the Reserve Bank could make advances at below market interest rates to finance long term infrastructure interventions. The Bank must lead the way in funding developmental investments that are aimed at addressing the historical backlogs in infrastructure and addressing apartheid inequalities.

The Reserve Bank should play a leading role in refinancing the budget and lowering the cost of borrowing of government – especially borrowing that is aimed at massive infrastructure rollout. The rationale for this is rooted in economics. When the state invests in massive infrastructure roll-out, it not only strengthens local procurement, but it also facilitates mass employment.

The amendment of the Reserve Bank Act will also make allowance for the state to be the sole shareholder on behalf of the people, and thus will guarantee the safeguarding of our sovereignty. Some private shareholders of the Bank are neither citizens of the Republic of South Africa nor do they reside in the country. While those who are not citizens cannot stand for election into the Board, they nonetheless do vote for Board representatives who ultimately govern the affairs of the Bank. The implication of this is that persons with no vested interests in the development of South Africa and her people outside their own personal accumulation through the increasing share value and influence of monetary policy, are making decisions for our country's future. This is an affront to the democracy we have fought for, which was fundamentally about the right to self-determine. But there can be no self-determination when your economic future rests in the hands of private individuals, some of whom are not citizens of the country.

As someone who is invested in global politics, which have shaped how you make sense of the future of coalition government, I am sure you have studied models of other Reserve Banks in the world. Is your argument in favour of the nationalisation of the central bank congruent with global practice?

Across the world, the number of central banks with private shareholders have declined over the years since the nationalisation of the Reserve Bank of Zealand. Most semi-developed and developed countries have state-owned and controlled central banks. Examples include England, Spain, New Zealand, India, Argentina, France, Portugal, Austria, and many other countries. The European Central Bank (ECB) represents another ownership model that is also state-centred. The Bank is established by treaty among EU member states. Besides the ECB, other supra-national central banks include the Eastern Caribbean Central Bank, the Bank of Central African States and the Central Bank of West African States.

The nationalisation of the Reserve Bank would thus align the South African Reserve Bank's ownership structure with most central banks across the world. There are pres-ently only eight countries in the world whose central banks have private shareholders. These are Turkey, Switzerland, Japan, Italy, Greece, San Marino, Belgium, and South Africa. But an important point must be emphasised. Although the central banks of Japan, San Marino, and Turkey have some private sector shareholders, the majority shareholder is still the state. In Belgium and Switzerland, around half of the shares are held by the government. By contrast, the Italian and South African governments have no formal ownership stake in their central banks.

Prior to the 2016 Local Government elections, you were the Deputy Minister of Trade and Industry. Why did you leave National Government to contest at Local Government?

The ANC is responsible for the deployment of its members to government and entities. We do not wake up and decide that we want to become Ministers, Deputy Ministers or Executive Mayors. It is the organisation, through its own wisdom, that decides where people must be placed based on their competencies. The ANC leadership determined that I should leave national politics and serve at local government level as the Executive Mayor of the City of Ekurhuleni and I had to abide by that determination. A disciplined member of the ANC knows that you go wherever you are sent. The same ANC that deploys you as a Minister can determine that you would better serve a branch, and you need to have the discipline to do so, because you must understand that you do not lead yourself, you are mandated by the organisation, which in turn is mandated by the people of South Africa.

Let's speak about the period leading up to the 2016 Local Government elections. There were indications even before the elections that the ANC was losing its hegemony in many parts of the country. Did you think the party would lose the Metros in Gauteng to the opposition?

When you have been involved in politics for as long as I have been, you develop an appreciation for the prevailing material conditions at any space and time. You also learn to read the thinking and the mood on the ground. It was evident to me and several other ANC leaders that the ground in the country and especially in the Gauteng Province had shifted significantly. There was a great deal of instability in all metros, emanating not only from citizens who were displeased with the performance of the ANC-led government in the province, but also from ANC members who felt alienated and unheard by the movement. The tensions were palpable, and the narrative was the same in all the metros as well as other municipalities across the country. In the third chapter of this book, I documented instances where the ANC was at war with itself – literally. Protests were happening at many provincial headquarters of the organisation and there was a great deal of disunity among us. In that sense, I knew that we were going to have an exceedingly difficult election. But to be honest, I don't think that I anticipated the extent of the haemorrhaging of support that the organisation suffered in that election and the 2019 national government election that followed. We must reflect honestly on the decline in support that the organisation battled with. It was devastating to witness, especially because the catastrophe was of our own making. The disunity leading up to the elections was far more severe than people realise – and the consequences were just as severe.

How were you feeling as you sat watching the election results coming in from the IEC?

It was an extremely difficult moment for all of us. In Gauteng it was especially brutal because the numbers were constantly neck-to-neck in all three metros. One minute it seemed like we would win it with an exceedingly small margin – the next minute it was the opposition in that situation. I was literally holding my breath and hoping that even if we did not win outright majorities, we would at least maintain strong plurality. But the minute we lost the City of Tshwane, I think I knew then that we were about to experience a bloodbath. And we did. It was devastating and I remember many dedicated ANC activists weeping at what they viewed as the annihilation of their political home.

At the 54th National Conference in Nasrec, the organisation adopted a unity framework. What necessitated this and is the framework still in place?

The idea of unity has always been the foundation on which the ANC is built. The formalisation of the unity framework in Nasrec was more a response to heightened divisions in the organisation than it was the birth of something completely new. It was Oliver Tambo who at the re-launch of the ANC Youth League inside the country, said: "We have survived these many decades of ruthless persecution because not once did we lose sight of the necessity for defending our unity. We can win our freedom by fostering maximum unity amongst our people." The ANC is the oldest national liberation movement in Africa and among the oldest in the world precisely because it has never lost sight of the importance of defending unity both internally and in society. The unity framework thus exists and continues to guide our organisational renewal ideals. There will always be those who work against unity because they benefit from division – this is true of the ANC and of society in general. There are people in this democratic dispensation who are still resistant to change because it benefits them to have a country that is fractured. But ours as the ANC remains a commitment to ensuring that we unite the organisation. And contrary to belief in some quarters that our talks of unity are disingenuous or opportunistic, we demonstrate every day that we are working towards uniting the organisation and country. In Ekurhuleni, for example, we are continuously engaging with disgruntled ANC members, some of whom left the organisation to join the opposition, to return and contribute to rebuilding the movement. To us, unity is not about political expediency – it is the foundation on which the future of the ANC lies. Building unity is fundamentally about defending our democracy and advancing an emancipatory future.

In the book you speak of the fracture that led to the ANC's loss of power in the 2016 Local Government elections. What contribution as the party's Ekurhuleni Chairperson are you currently making within the structures in helping the ANC heal itself as it still finds itself deeply fractured?

The ANC in Ekurhuleni is a dynamic, strong, and largely united organisation. As with any organisation, we have had our own fair share of tensions that impacted on unity, and the consequences of this were evident in our electoral fortunes in 2016. While we maintained plurality, the fact that we could not obtain a majority came down to the internal weaknesses of the organisation rather than the rejection of the organisation by voters. Having made this reflection when we assumed office, it was important to us to prioritise organisational renewal and the fostering of unity. This was achieved by creating platforms for engagement, where our differences could be honestly and critically engaged. We continue, to this day, to normalise a culture of open engagement with members of the organisation who hold different views. This has created an environment where members feel valued, and when people know they are valued, they become productive within the organisation – participating in branch, zonal and regional activities and initiatives that are aimed at mobilising and organising our communities. But this goes beyond the ANC. As the Regional Chairperson of the ANC in Ekurhuleni, I have also been very invested, along with the collective, in resolving some of the salient challenges within the broader Congress Movement. We are very engaged with the

Progressive Youth Alliance in the region, as well as other component structures, with whom we meet regularly to take stock of our progress and resolve our individual and collective problems.

In the Metsimaholo Local Municipality in the Free State, the South African Communist Party contested the ANC. There have also been tensions within the alliance over time. Do you think the alliance is still relevant?

The situation in Metsimaholo, as explained in Chapter three of this book, was a complex one. And while the November 2017 by-election in Metsimaholo cemented the reality that the ANC is bleeding there, the party did enough in each of the sixteen wards that it defended to prevail. We ended up winning sixteen of the forty-two seats. The SACP did not perform well at all. It failed to win a single ward in the twenty-one that it contested. Both results are devastating to me because they demonstrate that when the ANC and the SACP are divided, neither of them can emerge as the winner. This similar pattern can also be gleaned in higher learning institutions where divisions within the Progressive Youth Alliance tend to benefit opposition student organisations as opposed to the individual organisations within the alliance who contest each other.

In terms of the significance of the tripartite alliance, it is important to understand its historical basis and key objectives. The tripartite alliance is bound by ties that have existed for many decades. It was the 1955 Congress of the People that gave practical demonstration of the inherent ties between progressive anti-apartheid forces – the ANC and the Communist Party, as well as organised and unorganised workers. The SACP and COSATU have, since our liberation struggle, played an instrumental role in ensuring the realisation of the national democratic society to which the ANC is greatly committed. The ANC's and SACP's strategic pursuit of the national democratic revolution is not possible without the social transformation unionism of COSATU. This was evident in our electoral agenda in 1994 when we sought to annihilate apartheid hegemonic power and remains true to this day when we seek to redress the persistent legacy of our apartheid past. The SACP continues to inject a revolutionary consciousness in the ANC – something that is especially necessary as the ANC governs at a time when neo-liberal hegemony characterises global politics and economics. COSATU's mobilisation and organisation of workers is a crucial factor in why there is such high worker political consciousness in our country. Workers continue to identify a broad range of aspirations with the party, and it is for this reason that the organisation remains the primary figurehead of political and social change in these workers' political imaginations. The alliance is extremely important and all components in it are bringing to the table what they have a historical obligation to bring.

You were once appointed as the convenor of the ANC Youth League National Task Team. Today the YL is still led through an NTT, with no end in sight. Why is the YL struggling and what are the implications of this for the ANC going towards the 2021 Local Government elections, given the centrality of the youth vote?

The ANCYL has been going through an exceedingly difficult period over the past few years, heightened in part by some of the dynamics within the ANC that inherently have consequences for the league and other component structures of the mass democratic movement. Another factor has perhaps been the failure of the organisation to evolve with the times in terms of how it organises and mobilises. The ANCYL, like many organisations, has been unable to carve an identity in a space where political identities have become complex, and where representation therefore must reflect these complexities. I get the sense that the organisation is consistently speaking to itself rather than embracing the multiplicity of ideas and identities that exist. For example, if you read documents of the ANCYL on the gender question, you find that much of it still frames gender along binary lines that had always been used to frame the question. But the youth of today has discarded binary identities and embraces the multiplicity of identities that are continuously being developed, defined and re-defined. In this way, the YL alienates a significant proportion of youth that it could be mobilising under the banner of the ANC, which is one of its twin tasks.

But the YL is not dead even as it is going through a difficult period. There are countless voices that are still audible and making sense about what needs to happen to the organisation in order that it is shaped into the force it was once and can still be. Although I make it a point to not invest myself too intimately in the affairs of the YL since I believe young people must be given the space to exercise their collective agency, I do still engage with the organisation's developments, and I know that there is an intention to re-stabilise it, which is important for the ANC and the broader mass democratic movement, particularly as we go towards elections where we will need the youth to give legitimacy to our electoral ideals. If the YL is not stabilised, it will be exceedingly difficult for the ANC to capture the imagination of young people in a country that is largely comprised of the youth. The youth are a demographic dividend which, if not harnessed, will present significant problems for the ANC and the country.

What kinds of problems?

Problems that emerge when the youth feel alienated from politics. I read an interesting Master's thesis titled "From apartheid to democracy: A historical analysis of local struggles in Phomolong Township, Free State: 1985-2005" by activist and historian Phindile Kunene, in which she traces the evolution of local struggles in Phomolong Township, using service delivery protests to situate the history and context of local struggles that centre the role and functions of the local state. One of the many profound arguments that she poses is that at the forefront of these post-apartheid protests in Phomolong Township is working-class youth that has been hurled to the margins, socio-economically and politically, and which now lead these protests that are increasingly becoming violent as a response to the problems posed by the local state. Similar arguments are made by other researchers around the issue of the radicalisation of the youth that must be understood as a precursor to engaging in terrorist activities that pose a security and economic risk. When the youth is not engaged progressively, such problems and many others develop. It is especially important that we intervene.

Let's talk coalition governments. The City of Ekurhuleni has undoubtedly been the most stable Metro under a coalition government. What do you think are the ingredients of a successful coalition government?

The City of Ekurhuleni had to work extremely hard to ensure that we maintain a stable coalition government. Many people assume that the stability was natural, but it was in fact a product of dedicated efforts on the part of the ANC regional leadership and our coalition partners. From my experience, there are three particularly important ingredients that go into creating a stable coalition government. The first is that you need to enter a coalition with parties that have a common political interest, not merely a common ideological orientation. In the next chapter, Chapter six, on recommendations and the future of coalition governments, I explain the difference between the two. Parties that you go into a coalition with must want the same political outcomes as you do, otherwise you are going to have a lot of conflict. Take the example of the DA-led coalition in the City of Johannesburg. By the former Mayor's admission, his own party had different political interests to those of its coalition partners who were genuinely interested in structural transformation as opposed to the liberal reforms that were being proposed by the DA. It was inevitable, under such conditions, that the coalition would collapse. The second ingredient is consultation. A coalition government is a product and function of consultation – consultation is the glue that holds it together.

A total of twenty-nine monthly coalition meetings were convened between January 2017 and October 2020 in the City of Ekurhuleni. The purpose of these was to deliberate on pertinent issues related to governance. The ANC might have received the majority vote, but this must never be a basis to marginalise or undermine the smaller parties who bring fewer numbers to the coalition. Even a party that brings one seat to the coalition is extremely important because without that seat, there would be no government for the ANC to lead. So, the majority party within the coalition must make it a deliberate point to always consult with other coalition members on decisions affecting the Council. Secondly, there must be mutual respect by all partners, and none must be made to feel inadequate or in any way unimportant. In this book I have spoken a great deal about alienation and its devastating effects. It applies even in coalition governments. The third most important ingredient is transparency. One of the reasons that voters mandate a coalition to govern them is the belief that a coalition government is more transparent than one where a single party has complete hegemony. Whether this is true is a debate we can engage, but what is true is that transparency strengthens the social contract between government and the people. It gives legitimacy to that government. So, a coalition government must always act in a manner that is consistent with principles of accountability and transparency, which are at the heart of good governance.

In terms of governance, What has been the highlight for the coalition government in the City of Ekurhuleni?

We have maintained clean and unqualified audits over the past five years, with no unauthorised, irregular, or fruitless expenditure, and a clean audit on performance information. This is a testament of our commitment to good governance and sound financial management. It is also a result of deliberate and sustained efforts to rid the City of any form of corruption, maladministration, and misappropriation of funds, which have a catastrophic impact on our ability to deliver quality services to our people. Our Forensic Unit within the Internal Audit investigates any fraud, and corruption, non-compliance matters, instances of unauthorised, irregular, fruitless, and wasteful expenditure are also investigated. The outcomes of these investigations are reported to the Municipal Public Accounts Committee. Through these investigations, the City has managed to continuously achieve its objectives by improving the effectiveness of governance, risk management, and control processes.

What were the major obstacles in the establishment of the coalition government in Ekurhuleni and how did you deal with them?

Naturally, it was difficult to transition from having been the governing party to being part of a coalition government. Just at a psychological level, it is an extremely difficult transition to make. But when you understand that your primary objective is to serve your people, you realise that a bruised ego and hurt feelings are of no significance. You deal with that by internalising the fact that your mandate is to serve people and that this is still possible within the context of a coalition. Therefore, you work hard to strengthen and stabilise the coalition government – so that it can fulfil its mandate. And naturally, you are going to have some differences with your coalition partners – it happened even in the City of Ekurhuleni where the coalition was so strong. We differed about matters big and small. But what sustained our relationship was the first ingredient I mentioned: common political interests. All of us wanted to see the City work for our people, so we understood the importance of finding convergence on issues. The ANC won some debates, but it lost others, and this is what it means to be part of a coalition government.

Who benefits the most in a coalition government and what are those benefits?

The only people who are supposed to benefit from government are citizens. They are the primary stakeholders of government, along with businesses and other entities that contribute to the life of the country and the livelihoods of people. So, a good coalition government is one where the people are at the centre. Coalition partners must work together to ensure that whatever their differences may be, in the end analysis, the citizens that they are mandated to serve are not deprived of access to public services and other things that government must provide. Coalition governments are meant to benefit communities, because it's they who give the parties a mandate to govern. Politicians and administrators are public servants who must work for the people, so they cannot possibly be benefitting from government, be it a coalition or otherwise.

Unlike many ANC leaders who have often argued that the ANC needs to reclaim powerfully rather than go into coalitions, you believe that there is a future for them. Does this not place you at odds with your comrades?

The ANC, as I have often argued, is an organisation that is not resistant to different ideas blossoming and different schools of thought contending. It is one of the most profound features of the organisation and is perhaps one of the reasons why it has lived to be over a hundred years old. There is room for difference – it is the mark of genuine democracy.

And let me be clear, Mzilikazi, that my argument is not that the ANC should not aspire to govern. Rather, I am saying that we must be mentally and intellectually prepared for the eventuality of a change of politics – for the future realities of coalition governments. In the ANC, we prepared ourselves for democracy at a time when it did not seem possible that the White minority government would be defeated. Before we were even a governing party, we had drafted the Ready to Govern framework that detailed how we would go about with administration in a democratic South Africa. I am arguing for a similar thinking to find expression.

But don't you think coalition governments pose a significant threat to governing parties like the ANC?

I think coalition governments pose a significant opportunity for governing parties. The reality is that former national liberation movements cum governing parties are haemorrhaging electoral support. It is the reality in South Africa and everywhere across the continent and the world. The reasons are layered and complex and must be understood within both local and global contexts of the emergence of different kinds of politics. Governing parties, if they are to maintain their relevance, need to embrace these developments and position themselves in a way that will enable them to still impart great influence rather than be thrown into opposition benches where they will be denied room to negotiate legislative reforms and other things. You can see from our own experience in South Africa how difficult it can be for your ideas to find expression legislatively when you do not have adequate numerical backing in legislatures and the national assembly. But when governing parties, losing power, enter coalitions with progressive forces, they can ensure that they are still able to influence meaningful change.

So, you're saying coalitions are inevitable?

It is a mathematical certainty that at some point, coalition governments are going to define the nature of South African politics. It might not happen in these upcoming elections or the next, but at some point, we are going to have many local, district and metropolitan municipalities in our country being governed through coalitions and we need to have a solid framework for how we are going to ensure that these coalitions are stable and effective.

One of the problems that we have in Africa is the tendency to wait for things to happen before we start thinking seriously about them. Take industrial revolutions for example. We were left behind in all of them not only because of our historical experiences with colonialism and its disenfranchising nature, but because we also did not anticipate the changes that they would bring. The result was that the rest of the world defined them for us, and we were forced to transpose their practices that were often in conflict with our own realities, cultures and belief systems. We are not fully engaged in the Fourth Industrial Revolution and the result is that the West and China are defining it for us, sometimes out of context, and often without regard for our own realities. Machines are being programmed that do not recognise African faces, African languages, etc. The implications are terrible for us. This will happen with coalition governments too. We are going to find ourselves confronted with a new world in which politics is done differently, and if we do not invest in understanding that world and what our position in it must be, we are going to have serious problems.

Problems such as the collapse of government as was the case in the City of Tshwane?

Precisely. The idea that a country's capital city and one of its biggest metropolitan municipalities can find itself without an Executive Mayor, a Mayoral Committee, or a City Manager, and can be placed under administration, is unthinkable. And yet it happened in Tshwane because the coalition was so irreparably broken. The collapse of the coalition government in the administrative capital must serve as a warning of what will happen if we do not develop a framework or blueprint for how we must manage coalition governments.

Your research team visited Zimbabwe to gather information about the Government of National Unity (GNU) that was established in the country by the MDC and ZANU-PF in 2009. What were some of the surprising findings that you and your team made on this trip?

My research team did extensive work in Zimbabwe and with the Zimbabwean diaspora in South Africa and other parts of the region to understand the realities and legacies of the GNU. There were several findings that are elaborated on in Chapter two of this book. But for me, the most interesting finding is how opposition parties make sense of the GNU versus how the ordinary Zimbabwean on the streets does. Several leaders of the MDC-Alliance who were interviewed for this book indicated that they did not think that a GNU or coalition government would work in Zimbabwe, arguing that the governing ZANU-PF was atrophied beyond redemption. Those who worked in government during the GNU detailed how their ZANU-PF colleagues were constantly sabotaging initiatives and programmes proposed by the opposition coalition partner(s), and how difficult the experience of the GNU was. And yet, ordinary people who were interviewed argued that under the GNU, life was better in Zimbabwe than it had ever been, and that the economy was slowly beginning to recover from decades of collapse. People shared with us how their trust in state institutions was slowly regained, grounded in the knowledge that the MDC would hold the ZANU-PF accountable in government. These contrasting experiences interest me, and I think it is an area of discourse that needs greater work and research beyond Zimbabwe.

Does the future of Zimbabwe lie in another GNU?

I think the answers will differ depending on who you ask. If you ask ordinary Zimbabwean people, they will likely argue that in the absence of a complete overhaul of the political system, a GNU or coalition government would be greatly preferable. But if you ask the MDC-Alliance, the answer will be that there is no future for Zimbabwe with the ZANU-PF in it, and that the only way the country can be saved is for the party to be obliterated. ZANU-PF will argue that the MDC-Alliance is unfit to govern.

If you ask Mzwandile Masina?

If you ask me, I will say that every nation must self-determine. I am uncomfortable with the idea of a political leader of one country prescribing solutions for another country based on their own interpretations of what is happening in that country. I have my own ideas about what could be the problem in Zimbabwe, but it would be arrogant to then transpose solutions that we have implemented in South Africa to a Zimbabwe that has its own history and context. It would go against everything I stand for, which is fundamentally that the sovereignty of a country must be sacrosanct. It is at the heart of why I am advocating for the nationalisation of the South African Reserve Bank and stand opposed to the privatisation of the national carrier and other state-owned enterprises that many have argued ought to be sold to rid the state of their debt burden. But I do think that it would be important for Zimbabwe, like South Africa, to re-think the nature of its politics. Zimbabwe is not an island; it is part of a global village in which politics are evolving and coalitions are proving to be a new way of governing. It is probably more important for Zimbabwe to think deeply about this given its contemporary struggles, at the centre of which is the crisis of legitimacy that the ZANU-PF government is contending with. But the issue must go beyond Zimbabwe and South Africa. African countries in their entirety must engage with the question of the future realities of coalition governments, because the political milieu is not what it was twenty years ago and the generation of voters that is emerging is not going to be won through tales of the memory of colonialism and White minority rule. It is a reality that needs to be confronted with an open mind and an eagerness to dare to re-imagine a different civilisation.

Which, in your opinion, is the best model for coalition governments in the world?

There are several models that have been developed and are being implemented across the world. In the developed world, I think Germany certainly presents the world with one of the best models. The current government of Germany under Chancellor Angela Merkel and Federal President Frank-Walter Steinmeier is made of a coalition of the Christian Democratic Union (CDU), the Christian Social Union of Bavaria (CSU), and the Social Democratic Party (SPD). In terms of the composition of the cabinet, the coalition government is proportionally represented. The cabinet consists of Chancellor Angela Merkel and fifteen federal ministers – seven of whom are from the CDU, six from the SPD and three from the CSU. The parliament of Germany, called the Bundestag, is elected directly by voters. Elections use a mixed-member proportional representation system which combines first-past-the-post elected seats with a proportional party list. This has worked very well for Germany, maintaining both its democracy and ensuring that strong systems are in place to keep government functioning. The coalition government in Germany is extremely strong and has seen Germany maintain its status as the biggest national economy in Europe and the fourth largest in the world.

Evidence before us suggests that when a coalition government is unstable as is the case in the City of Tshwane and Nelson Mandela Bay Metro, it is the citizens who suffer. But what are the rewards that citizens reap in a stable coalition government like the one you are leading?

When a coalition is stable and government is working, it is evident in the results of service delivery. I can give just one example on a service where the coalition government in the City of Ekurhuleni had a common vision and the results were great. Our coalition has always been focused on implementing human capital development interventions on behalf of community members. The provision of financial assistance is one of the many initiatives that the City is implementing to achieve its goal of increasing the skills base of the region. Such interventions can only happen when there is a common vision in a coalition – when we all value the same things for our people, which in this case was education for the youth of our municipality.

What lessons must we learn from the failed coalition governments in the Metros?

The most important lesson that the instability of coalitions in the City of Tshwane, the City of Johannesburg and the Nelson Mandela Bay Metro has taught us is that an unstable coalition is extremely costly for the people. Evidence suggests that when coalitions are unstable, service delivery is greatly affected. In the case of the City of Tshwane, in the 2019/2020 financial year, the capital expenditure was less than 30 percent. This means that in that financial year, the metro carried out extraordinarily few development projects. These are at the heart of economic growth and development without which there can be no attraction of foreign direct investment or any investment at all, which we know goes where there is infrastructure development. When there is no investment and therefore limited resources for a municipality, it is the citizens who suffer because services cannot be delivered to them, and development that could aid in their livelihood generation cannot happen. It is a devastating scenario.

Another important lesson that we must learn is that political parties with fundamentally different ideological stances and political interests will not manage a successful coalition. There was just no possible way that a liberal DA that is committed to preserving White privilege could survive working with an EFF that sits on the extreme opposite side of the spectrum. For coalitions to work, there needs to be a common political interest. Without this, there will be constant in-fighting and conflict that will result in the collapse of government which, as I argue in my first point, has catastrophic implications for the people.

You contend that the EFF is not a class enemy of the ANC, but merely its opposition. Does this mean you believe that the ANC and EFF could co-govern through a coalition?

The EFF is not a class enemy of the ANC. The PAC is not a class enemy of the ANC. AZAPO is not a class enemy of the ANC. These are organisations that are part of what we refer to as progressive forces – organisations which, even as we might not have the same ideological and philosophical leanings, are equally committed to the pursuit of a cause for the emancipation of the disenfranchised and marginalised people in our country. These are parties that we are in opposition with for the contestation of state power, but they are not parties that we can reasonably define as our class enemies because the motive force of their struggle is no different to ours at a fundamental level. Parties like the Freedom Front Plus and the DA, whose interest is in protecting minority interests and who are resistant to radical economic transformation are the ones who are our class enemy, because where we seek to liberate the poor working-class majority, they seek to maintain the status quo where the capitalist class is the symbol of power and continues to maintain ownership and control of the means of production. For this reason, I believe that the EFF and the ANC could find common ground and govern together. There have been instances when the parties have found common ground, such as with the question of subjecting section 25 of the Constitution to a review to set parameters for the expropriation of land without compensation, which is a conference resolution of both parties. We also find convergence in issues such as free education, universal access to healthcare, etc. I think the EFF, PAC, AZAPO and such parties ought to be the natural choice for a coalition for the ANC.

I doubt that the EFF would want to go into a coalition with the ANC when it has made it clear throughout its existence that it wants to remove the party from power, and refused to give it votes that could have kept the Metros in the hands of the ANC

That is a fair point, but I also think that one of the marks of a political party's progressiveness is the ability to read material conditions correctly and to respond appropriately. The global rise of right-wing politics that saw the election of leaders such as Donald Trump in the USA and many other right-wing governments in Europe, Latin America, and parts of the world, has had a significant impact on our own politics. The performance of right-wing parties in our own country, such as the Freedom Front Plus that saw a significant increase in electoral support in both the 2016 local government and 2019 national elections, does not bode well for the future of our country and its democracy. I think the EFF understands what is at stake if progressive forces do not unite to undermine this right-wing onslaught. So, I do think that there is room for the ANC and the EFF to find one another. But it is a conversation that needs to happen at a national level between the national leaderships of the two parties.

If the City of Ekurhuleni were to be thrust into another coalition government at the upcoming Local Government elections, would you enter a coalition with the same partners you are in it with now?

The City of Ekurhuleni was extremely fortunate to have a coalition government comprised of political parties that have a common political interest in so far as wanting to make the City work for the citizens of Ekurhuleni. We were committed, from the very first day, to this pursuit. As our administration draws to a close, I can confidently say that we have managed to sail through turbulent waters and to emerge stronger and united. The ANC is certainly aiming to contest state power and to win the election with a clear majority – that has never been a debate. We are working extremely hard to ensure that we win the metro with a convincing majority. However, should the situation repeat itself, and we again find ourselves needing to establish a coalition government, there is absolutely no doubt that the political parties that we worked with will be engaged to form part of the coalition. They have demonstrated immeasurable commitment to the common cause of creating a better life for all and have never made us question this commitment. There is no reason why we would not work together again, all things being equal.

Should the OR Tambo School of Leadership that has done significant intellectual work in teaching members of the ANC around matters of organisational history, discipline, handling of factionalism, battles of ideas, etc., consider designing a curriculum on future realities of coalition governments in South Africa?

The OR Tambo School of Leadership is a particularly important instrument in the hands of not only members of the ANC, but the broader progressive and democratic movement. Just looking at the composition of its Board of Directors, which comprises not only some of the greatest stalwarts and intellectuals in the movement, but also young activists who are shaping South Africa's polity, evidences the institution's commitment to building agents of change with a well-rounded worldview. The school is a battleground of ideas that challenge the ANC to be a relevant and better organisation. The school's enabling of an environment of debate is rooted deeply in ANC traditions. The culture of debate and disagreement is at the heart of what makes the ANC a truly democratic organisation.

Different schools of thought must contend, and we must not shy away from disagreeing with one another provided that these disagreements are not elevated above the ideals and aspirations of the organisation. Factionalism is born not out of different perspectives or ideas, but out of the destructive belief that the organisation must subordinate itself to these differences. The OR Tambo School of Leadership, in embedding ANC traditions in us, is teaching us to recognise that difference is necessary only in so far as it strengthens the organisation rather than weakens it, which is what factionalism does.

Beyond educating ANC members about the history and traditions of the organisation, it also provides practical tools for the development of cadres who understand social, economic, political, and philosophical concepts that enable analysis of contemporary local and global society from a transformation perspective, through continuous assessment in classes and course modules. But it also provides tools for ANC public representatives, ensuring that revolutionary principles that include discipline permeate into all institutions in which ANC members are located or deployed. I cannot think of a better institution to lead the charge of aiding in the development of a framework for coalition governments as we head towards the 2021 local government elections.

Would you participate in the drafting of this framework, given your experience in governing in a coalition?

It is my greatest hope that while this book might not provide all the answers needed about how to govern in a coalition, it will at least spark conversation around the present and future realities of coalition governments in South Africa. Capturing the experiences of those who were instrumental in the establishment of these coalition governments, including those that failed, is my way of highlighting what the pitfalls of this kind of government are, and what needs to be done differently next time around. In this sense, I want to believe that I have inadvertently participated in the drafting of this framework. Of course, there is still more work that needs to be done, particularly in the ANC where this discussion has not found root. A lot of it is the work of imagining society anew, and it is not the kind of work that can be achieved with one book. It is, however, work that demands commitment to the ideational space, to understanding global politics and, importantly, to recognising shifts in the thinking and imaginations of the electorate in South Africa. I also hope that students of public administration and local government will be encouraged to study the subject much more deeply and perhaps come up with better ideas for how our country can make sense of coalitions and develop innovative and advanced models for their sustainability and stability. Hopefully, this will all happen in time before the upcoming local government elections – so that we do not commit the same mistakes as we did before.

6

REFLECTIONS AND RECOMMENDATIONS

Empirical evidence from the South African political milieu and the world suggests that coalition governments are becoming a reality of our politics. The plurality that the ANC maintained in the local, district and metropolitan municipalities where it lost power to opposition indicates that there are still millions of people who believe in the party. Results from by-elections also give an indication that the party is slowly reclaiming power in some wards that it had initially lost. Whether this could mean that the upcoming local government elections will see the party reclaim power and cease to govern through coalitions in metropolitan municipalities is yet to be seen. But my assessment is that even if it is going to reclaim power, the wins will be by exceedingly small margins as opposed to the overwhelming majorities that were attained in the earlier years of democracy. The 2016 local government elections changed the political field forever. South African politics will never be the same again even if the ANC retains the lost metros. It is a mathematical certainty that at some point, coalitions are going to become a norm. Power in a democracy is never lost absolutely – it is always lost in pockets. This is what we are seeing with the ANC and with all other former national liberation movements cum governing parties in democracies across Africa and the world. The idea of a single political party enjoying electoral hegemony is no longer sustainable and the reasons for this vary.

Evolution of National Liberation Movements

On the African continent, we are seeing a significant decline in support for former national liberation movements. The haemorrhaging of electoral support that the ANC experienced in the previous local government and general elections is not unique even as it is concerning to us as ANC leaders and members. It is a universal trend across the continent, and in many ways, the ANC is better positioned than most former national liberation movements that have been relegated to opposition benches nationally or, in the case of the ZANU-PF in Zimbabwe, that have been stripped of legitimacy by elections deemed neither free nor fair by observers and other institutions.

There are numerous theories about why former national liberation movements on the continent experience sharp declines in support in the second decade of independence. Southall (2013) argues that this has to do with the evolution of liberation movements. According to this perspective, the making of a new nation as was required by transitions from colonialism or minority rule entailed the deliberate construction of a historical memory of how the nation had been forged and how it was to imagine itself. The process, he argues, has been an incoherent and extremely messy one. A part of this has to do with the fact that national liberation movements themselves emerged out of messy processes and were not necessarily strong beyond their organising power to overthrow the oppressive regimes. Liberation struggles everywhere in the world arose out of necessity and as a last resort in the fight against minority or colonial rule. They often followed decades of other modes of struggle such as defiance campaigns, as was the case with South Africa. Such campaigns were often non-violent in nature, and necessarily had to be because colonial and minority states enjoyed a monopoly on violence. The implication of this is that national liberation movements had limited ability to operate optimally, forcing organising and mobilisation to happen unconventionally and without some necessities.

This is perhaps one of the most uncomfortable conversations within national liberation movements cum governing parties, but it is a conversation that demands critical reflection. ANC stalwart Khulu Mbatha laid the ground for this conversation in *Unmasked: Why the ANC Failed to Govern*, when he asked how prepared the organisation was to govern and whether it understood the nature of the global and local economy, and what they meant for South Africa's economic future. While I do not agree with most of the arguments that are posed by Mbatha, I do think that there is value in reflecting on the holistic preparedness of men and women who had spent decades in the trenches waging armed struggles, dominated by a racial group that had, for centuries, been systematically excluded from the economy and dispossessed of the means of production, and whose practice of democracy did not emerge organically due to the space and time in which they organised, to govern newly democratised countries.

While I do not agree with most of the arguments that are posed by Mbatha, I do think that that there is value in reflecting on the holistic preparedness of men and women to govern newly democratised countries after spending decades in the trenches waging an armed struggle against a racial group that had, for centuries, systematically excluded them from the economy and dispossessed them of the means of production, and whose practice of democracy did not emerge organically due to the space and time in which they organised.

This reflection ought not to be done as a means of vindicating the bigoted idea that Black leaders were and are incapable of governing, but as a means of assessing how some commitments and decisions made at the dawn of our democracy were inherently impossible. These impossibilities continue to haunt the democratic government, which on one hand seeks to redress injustices of the past and provide a life of value for everyone in South Africa, and on the other, must contend with the real limitations of political power in a neo-liberal global order.

Another factor is the embeddedness of colonialism, about which Public Affairs Professor Mashupye Maserumule argues that the fundamentals of the apartheid colonial social order are still in place, with the democratic regime unwittingly administering them. Maserumule (2015) contends that there has not been a meaningful challenge to the "colonial matrices of power", which have placed great impediments to the construction of the post-apartheid state. He goes on to argues that these matrices "foster institutional racism based on Hegelianism – a body of thought that characterises the cognitive faculty of Africans as, in Senegalese philosopher Souleymane Diagne's words, in *The Meaning of Timbuktu*, the "other reason and philosophical spirit" is bereft of the "capacity to think and live by a consistent system of sound principles". The implication of this is that the defeat of colonialism in Africa has not translated to the annihilation of coloniality. The latter finds expression in some of our public administration and management practices that are slowing down the pace of meaningful transformation. This then translates into unfulfilled promises by governing parties which, as national liberation movements, made bold commitments that were at odds with the material realities of governance, about what they would deliver. But a hungry mother living in an informal settlement, who registered for an RDP house in 1998, does not understand nor is she interested in the red tape that makes it impossible to simply allocate a newly built house to her. Neither does a young man interested in farming understand the processes that the state must undertake to avail arable land – which unfortunately include the purchase of such land from a private owner, usually a White man, and transfer of the land to the state for determination of use. These factors, among others, inform roaring support for former national liberation movements on the eve of post-independence and democracy, and the dying support decades later.

The Character of South African Political Parties

Making sense of the experiences of coalition governments in South Africa demands honest reflections from key role players who were instrumental in the establishment and collapse of the coalitions. Coalition governments are neither easy nor rapid to establish. There is much work that goes into establishing coalitions, particularly in a South Africa wherein hundreds of political organisations contest elections. The 2016 local government elections were contested by over two hundred political parties – a similar number contested the 2019 general elections three years later. One of the hurdles that must be crossed is that of determining whether there is significant alignment in political interests – which is not always true even for political parties that may appear to have similar philosophies. A clear example of this can be gleaned with the Workers and Socialist Party (WASP) and the Marxist Workers Party that was established in 2019.

The issue of having hundreds of political parties contesting for state power demands reflection. There are two opposing schools of thought in this regard. Some argue that having many parties on the ballot is a sign of a healthy democracy while others argue that it sets parameters for its weakening. There is a degree of validity to both arguments. Because of South Africa's history of colonialism and apartheid, democracy is our most valued asset. For many decades, the Black majority in this country was denied the right to vote for a government of their choice. The White minority government instituted many laws that made it impossible for Black, Coloured, Indian, and other Asian groups to participate meaningfully in the election of their own public representatives. This disenfranchisement was legitimised with the argument that persons who did not have assets, or a certain level of formal education, could not reasonably vote. It deliberately ignored the fact that Black people in their majority could not own assets because of centuries of land and economic dispossession by a White settler minority; and that policies of separate development meant that Black people could not have the same quality of education as their White counterparts. Kepe and Ntsebeza (2011) explain how the de-agrarianisation of Black people forced them into a migrant proletariat class that had to work for wages. In this way, Black people were alienated not only from the very assets that sustained their livelihoods, but that could have also given them the requisite social and economic status demanded for them to be eligible for voting.

Throughout the apartheid era, laws were passed that made both political participation and mobilisation almost impossible for the oppressed majority. The political disen-franchisement of Black people, although already happening by then, was cemented in 1960 following the devastating Sharpeville Massacre. The massacre, in which police fired at unarmed protesters in the township of Sharpeville in the Vaal, resulted in the killing of sixty-nine people and the wounding of hundreds more. A report would later reveal that over seven hundred bullets had been fired, all by police, and that many of the deceased were shot in the back while fleeing. The massacre was one of the most violent responses by the apartheid government to protest action. It also led to the banning of the ANC and the PAC under the Unlawful Organisations Act No 34 of 1960, which came into effect just two weeks after the massacre. The Communist Party had been banned a decade earlier under the Suppression of Communism Act of 1950. The unbanning of these political organisation would only happen in 1990 during the nego-tiations for the ending of apartheid – four years before South Africa would hold its first democratic elections.

It is evident why the issue of universal suffrage is so important to South African people – and therefore why to some, the participation of hundreds of political parties in elections is celebrated as something progressive. Centuries of being denied the right to assembly and to self-determination make the freedom of association even more profound. It is a mark of our collective march towards freedom – freedom for which many paid the ultimate price. And yet, empirical evidence suggests that the participation of so many parties in elections can have problematic implications, including the further fragmentation of society. Regional parties tend to work for the development of a particular region or for the growth of a linguistic, ethnic, tribal, religious, or even racial group only, to the disregard of the larger interests of other sections of society.

One of the complex realities laid bare by the multitudes of political parties that register with the Independent Electoral Commission in every election in our country is that similar (and sometimes even identical) political philosophy and ideology do not necessarily always translate to common political interests. It is possible and highly likely for political parties with the same philosophical and ideological orientations to not harbour the same political goals – and for their understanding of the aim of state power to be greatly different. One of the reasons for this occurrence is that for every political philosophy and ideology, there are multiple streams and interpretations.

That a party characterises itself as African nationalist does not necessarily imply that it interprets African nationalism in the same way as another that also characterises itself as such. This is evident with the ANC and the PAC, which both identify as African nationalist organisations but whose interpretation of Africanism is diametrically opposed. Perhaps an even more vivid example of this reality is that of the Inkatha Freedom Party (IFP) which, from its very inception in 1975 (at the time known as Inkatha YeSizwe), has always characterised itself as an "all-embracing national movement with its sights set on the liberation of all South Africans" – an almost exact characterisation to that of the ANC, which had in 1955 declared itself an all-embracing movement committed to the idea that "South Africa belongs to all those who live in it – Black and White" as espoused in the Freedom Charter. And yet, in posture and orientation, historically and in the contemporary epoch, the ANC and IFP are two vastly different organisations with different political interests. Some brief points of divergence will be analysed.

At the height of the liberation struggle when it was abundantly clear that freedom would only be attained through armed struggle, the ANC and other national liberation movements including the PAC committed themselves to taking up arms. They went underground and sent their members for training across the continent and the Union of the Soviet Socialist Republics (USSR). The IFP, on the other hand, refused to engage in armed struggle – a position it affirms on its official website, stating: "Its emergence was a result of a desperate need at that time for black democratic forces to come to the fore and pick up the gauntlet of the black liberation struggle which had been left tragically destitute by so many others. Inkatha, however, remained firm in their rejection of the armed struggle". This posture by the IFP, as well as its evident collaboration with the apartheid government at the zenith of the liberation struggle, would forever define it as outside the fold of the progressive left movement that includes such organisations as the PAC and the Azanian People's Organisation (AZAPO).

These intricacies may appear somewhat trivial and some may even argue that as living organisms, political organisations are in a constant state of evolution, always changing to reflect evolving material conditions. It would even be true of the ANC, which has in over a century of its existence had its posture influenced by politics of time and space. But the histories of political organisations are not ignored when coalitions are established: who is defined as a progressive force and as a class enemy has an important bearing on how coalitions are formed. But making sense of this demands more than simply an understanding of history – it also requires subjective interpretations and experiences of government practitioners who are involved in the process of establishing coalitions. It is for this reason that a critical component in the writing of this book was lengthy interviews and engagements with men and women who led and are still part of coalitions across the country.

Class Enemies vs Opponent

One of the most important discussions born out of the outcomes of the 2016 local government elections and the subsequent unstable coalitions that followed is that of what the significant difference is between a class enemy and an opponent. This heightened the conflicts between the DA and EFF in DA-led coalitions that the EFF had supported. The political differences that emerged between the two organisations were not merely about a different approach to issues. It was not simply a question of differing tactics. The differences were rooted in the very ideological and philosophical leanings of the two parties. Whereas the DA is a liberal party, the EFF is a Socialist party whose ideas of how to liberate society differ radically from those of the DA. The differences are not subtle, they are as glaring as the differences between a dalmatian and a rottweiler. The two are, in a true sense of the word, class enemies. Class enemies refer to organisations whose ideological postures are on opposite ends of the spectrum, and whose motive force is different. The motive force of the DA's struggle is a White minority and a bourgeoisie that exists for the purpose of exploiting the motive force of the EFF's struggle: poor working-class people of African descent. That a coalition could have worked between the two was improbable and the tensions inevitable.

An opponent, on the other hand, refers to a political party of similar ideological and philosophical leanings with whom one is contesting for state power. The ANC is not a Socialist organisation, but it does have a bias towards working-class people. It is an organisation that is deeply invested in the pursuit of a national democratic society that can only be realised when the historically oppressed Black majority is economically, politically, socially, and culturally emancipated. The ANC and EFF thus have the same motive force, as does the SACP, AZAPO, PAC, AIC, WASP, BLF, SOPA, and other progressive forces. There are significant differences in terms of the strategies and tactics that these organisations employ. There are also differences in how these organisations make sense of certain political realities. But at a fundamental level, they are in pursuit of a remarkably similar if not a wholly identical struggle. They are, thus, political opponents.

Being able to determine who is a class enemy and who is an opponent is crucial in the context of forming coalition governments. These governments rise or fall on this one thing. It is not an accident of history that the breakdown between the EFF and DA in Nelson Mandela Bay Municipality was not anything that transpired in the said Council, but a decision by the DA in the National Assembly to vote against the EFF's proposition for the review of the Constitution. Ideological divergence that happened at national level greatly impacted relations at local level precisely because ideological leanings are the bedrock on which organisations are built. The ANC, which has its own differences with the EFF, voted with the organisation on this motion – a clear demonstration of how there is ideological convergence between the two organisations. An important lesson for all parties as we approach the 2021 local government elections is that for coalitions to work and to enjoy the stability that was seen in the City of Ekurhuleni, it is imperative that the partners are political opponents rather than class enemies. The differences that coalition partners must contend with should be about how to go about doing things, not what those things ought to be. There should be no doubt that all parties have the same political objective and a common interest, not merely a common enemy.

The Necessity of Coalition Governments

The main objective of this book was two-fold. Firstly, it was to capture the experiences of coalition governments in local, district and metropolitan municipalities in the period 2016–2021. This was done to make sense of what led to these coalitions and how they fared in terms of projecting a new imagination of South Africa's party-political system. Secondly, the book sought to lay foundations for an urgent conversation about what coalition governments must (and must not) look like, and their future realities in South Africa and the broader African continent. Much scholarly work needs to go into the study of coalition governments in our country and the entirety of the developing world so that we may understand what benefits our people can derive from stable and effective coalitions. I never pretended to have all the answers even as I am a government practitioner, activist, and someone with experience of being part of a coalition government. But I do hope that we can apply ourselves in reflecting on what the future of our country and its politics looks like – and whether we can mitigate the problems that we experienced in the metros by developing a universal framework for coalition governments of the future. These are inevitable, for the world is evolving and with it, our understanding and experience of government and public affairs.

In concluding this submission, I wish to reflect on this statement by United Nations Development Programme Senior Adviser in the Asia Pacific, G. Pramod Kumar, on the necessity of coalition governments in India:

> ...For a country that's constitutionally defined as a union of states, a federal government must also reflect the reality of a union of states that are socio-culturally, politically, and demographically diverse. A slice of India from any part of the country doesn't represent this diversity except when all the states are thrown in together. That's what a coalition of parties do (sic). Whether it's the BJP-led NDA or the Congress-led UPA, the regional parties bring in that element of Indian diversity. In a world where decentralisation is increasingly seen as an integral element of democracy, a single national party that doesn't have equal play in all the states, representing the whole of India is an anomaly. Regional parties and coalitions help the states claim their rightful position in the Union of India. In the erstwhile era of the top-down national governments, mostly dominated by the Congress since independence, Delhi called the shots. Despite the national, state, and concurrent subjects that ensured the division of jurisdiction of government under a federal system, the Centre always usurped the states' rights and even toppled inconvenient state governments at the drop of a hat. However, since the 1990s, the tables have been turned. The regional parties have marginalised national parties in many states and the decisions are moving away from Delhi. In fact, this is how it should be. That's where the world is moving towards, internationally decentralisation of power is increasingly seen as a mark of democratic governance. Many big countries such as Indonesia have embarked on decentralisation drives where the provinces and local governments decide policies and programmes that concern the people...
> (G. Pramod Kumar, World Bank Blogs)

Kumar aptly captures the economic and socio-political factors for why coalition governments exist and the important role they can play. But for this to happen, coalition governments must be stable and effective. The lesson that we learned in the post-2016 local government elections was that the inability to develop a working strategy for managing coalitions has the potential to spell disaster for ordinary people who rely on their local government to provide important services. We saw in Nelson Mandela Bay Metro how important resources were withheld by the National Treasury due to the instabilities of the coalition. We saw how service delivery was greatly compromised in the City of Tshwane by coalition battles. In Metsimaholo Local Municipality, the inability to approve a budget had a devastating effect on service delivery for the people. Evidently, where there is no stability, coalitions collapse. And where coalitions collapse, those hardest hit are the voters. For this reason, it is important that a framework is developed to inform how coalitions should be established and managed.

The following are recommendations that were made by the Ekurhuleni Region to the ANC Gauteng Local Government Summit, presented by the Chief Whip of the City of Ekurhuleni Council, Jongizizwe Dlabathi, which I believe must be the bedrock on which parties craft coalition policies. The recommendations, aimed at strengthening coalition management, are as follows:

1. Develop a clearly defined, well understood, and commonly accepted Coalition Agreement.
2. Craft the agreed upon governance principles in a manner that is consistent with those of the leading party in the coalition.
3. In terms of unwritten commitments, the leading party should commit on the minimum and confine them to what is possible.
4. Set a principle that will discourage the "regular coalition party expectations" above that which constitutes the primary Coalition Agreement.
5. The leading party must be consultative and engage and involve coalition partners in decision making. Additionally, it should take them into confidence and share its perspective on issues.
6. Establish coalition accountability platforms. These must include coalition summits and party-to-party strategic engagements.

That the future of South African politics is coalition governments is inevitable. The important thing to do now is to plan for this eventuality because if we fail to do so, we run the risk of history repeating itself with collapsed coalitions and metros being placed under administration. This is a lose-lose situation for all, but especially for South African people to whom government owes unwavering commitment.

———————————

REFERENCES

Areff, A. 2018. "We are cutting the throat of whiteness" – Malema on plans to remove Trollip. *News24*. Available at: https://www.news24.com/news24/South Africa/News/we-are-cutting-the-throat-of-white ness-malema-on-plans-to-remove-trollip-20180304. Accessed 2 October 2020.

Banya, N. 2008. Khama to boycott summit if no Zimbabwe deal. *Reuters*. Available at: https://www. reuters.com/article/uk-zimbabwe-crisis-idUKWEA6 08420080814. Accessed 30 April 2020.

Booysen, S. 2014. Causes and impact of party alliances and coalitions on the party system and national cohesion in South Africa. *Journal of African Elections*, 13(1):66-92.

Botha, S. 2004. Ten years of democracy: Characteristics of, and changes in, South Africa's party system. *Politeia*, 23(3):39-59.

Britannica Encyclopaedia. 2021. Elections. Available at: https://www.britannica.com/topic/election-political-science. Accessed 20 March 2020

BusinessTech. 2015. ANC could lose 'several important cities' in 2016. Available at: https://businesstech. co.za/news/government/107449/anc-could-lose-several-important-cities-in-2016/. Accessed 28 December 2020.

Cervenka, Z. 1987. The effects of militarization of Africa on human rights. Paper for Conference on Human Rights in the African Context. Published by Nordiska Afrikainstitutet.

Chander, J.N. 2004. Coalition politics: The Indian experience. New Dehli: Concept Publishing Company.

City of Johannesburg. 2018. The City of Johannesburg marks two years since a multi-party coalition government was formed at the last local government elections. Available at: https://www.joburg.org. za/media_/Newsroom/Pages/2018%20News%20 Articles/Mayor-Mashaba-administration-marks-2-years-in-multi-party-coalition-government.aspx. Accessed 15 August 2020.

City Press. 2013. Gauteng ANC ran ahead of themselves with Mbeki statement – Mantashe. *City Press*. 30 September.

Cuneo, C.N., Sollom, R. & Beyrer, C. 2017. The cholera epidemic in Zimbabwe, 2008-2009: A review and critique of the evidence. *Health and Human Rights Journal*, 19(2):249-264.

Dabengwa, D. 2017. Relations between ZAPU and the USSR, 1960s-1970s: A personal view. *Journal of Southern African Studies*, 43(1):215-223.

De Klerk, A. & Kgosana, K. 2018. DA plan to quit EFF coalitions fails to win party's backing. *Sunday Times*. 2 September.

Disch, L. 2002. *The tyranny of the two-party system*. New York: Columbia University Press.

Doherty, I. 2004. Coalition Best Practices. NDI West bank and Gaza. National Democratic Institute for International Affairs

Doran, S. 2017. *Kingdom, power, glory: Mugabe, Zanu and the quest for supremacy, 1960-1987*. Midrand: Sithatha Media.

EISA. 2008. *Zimbabwe: Post-harmonised election violence in April 2008*. African Democracy Encyclopaedia Project.

Electoral Institute for Sustainable Democracy in Africa. 2008. Election Observer Mission Report: The Zimbabwe Harmonised Elections of 29 March 2008. Available at: https://www.eisa.org/pdf/zimomr08.pdf.

eNCA. 2016. POLLS: DA maintains strong lead in Nelson Mandela Bay. Available at: https://www. enca.com/south-africa/polls-da-holds-strong-lead-in-nelson-mandela-bay. Accessed 21 August 2020.

Engel, U. 2016. Zupta's next nightmare: The South African Local Government Elections of 3 August 2016. *Africa Spectrum*, 51(2):103-115. Available at: https:// nbn-resolving.org/urn:nbn:de:gbv:18-4-9809.

Feketha, S. 2019. Herman Mashaba: Why I am resigning from the DA. *Independent*. Available at: https://www.iol.co.za/news/politics/herman-mashaba-why-i-am-resigning-from-the-da-35508920. Accessed 10 January 2021.

George, Z. 2013. Numsa breaks official link with ANC alliance. *Daily Dispatch*. 23 December.

Government of the Republic of South Africa. 2020. Hawks pounce on Nelson Mandela Bay corruption case suspects. *SA Government News Agency*. Available at: https://www.sanews.gov.za/south-africa/hawks-pounce-nelson-mandela-bay-corruption-case-suspects. Accessed 12 January 2021.

Greffrath, W. & Van der Waldt, G. 2016. Section 139 interventions in South African local government, 1994-2015. *New Contree*, 75:135-160.

Grobler, R. & AFP. 2019. Xenophobic violence: Mashaba says he has 'nothing to apologise for'. *News24*. Available at: https://www.news24.com/news24/SouthAfrica/News/xenophobic-violence-mashaba-says-he-has-nothing-to-apologise-for-20190918. Accessed 24 August 2020.

Hegel, W. 1967. *Philosophy of Right*. London: Oxford University Press.

Hlahla, P. 2013. Sasolburg residents defiant on merger. *Pretoria News*. 31 January.

Human Rights Watch. 2008. Bullets for each of you: State-sponsored violence since Zimbabwe's March 29 Elections. Available at: https://www.hrw.org/report/2008/06/09/bullets-each-you/state-sponsored-violence-zimbabwes-march-29-elections. Accessed 1 May 2020.

Human Rights Watch. 2008. All over again: Human rights abuses and flawed electoral conditions in Zimbabwe's coming general elections. PDF. Available at: https://www.hrw.org/reports/2008/zimbabwe0308/.

Hyug Baeg, 1991. Hegemony and Counter-Hegemony In Gramsci. *Asian Perspective*, 15(1):123-156.

IEC. 2016. Results Summary. Available at: https://www.elections.org.za/content/LGEPublicReports/197/Deatiled%20Results/GP.pdf. Accessed 27 April 2020.

Independent Electoral Commission. 2016. *2016 local government elections report*. IEC.

Independent News. 2003. "Puppet of the West deserves jail" – Mugabe. Available at: https://www.iol.co.za/news/africa/puppet-of-the-west-deserves-jail-mugabe-108111.

Inkatha Freedom Party. Available at: https://www.ifp.org.za/who-we-are/our-history/. Accessed 10 November 2020.

Institute for Security Studies. 2016. Fact Sheet: SA's 2014/15 sexual crime statistics. Eyewitness News. Available at: https://ewn.co.za/2015/10/02/FACTSHEET-SAs-2014-15-assault-and-sexual-crime-statistics. Accessed 27 September 2020.

International Crisis Group. 2013. *Zimbabwe: Election scenarios*. Johannesburg: ICG.

Jackson-Nudelman, M. 2020. The two-party system fails American voters. *Pipe Dream*. Available at: https://www.bupipedream.com/opinions/117576/auto-draft-316/. Accessed 12 December 2020.

Jo'burg Media. 2018. Mayor Mashaba administration marks 2 years in multi-party coalition government. Available at: https://www.joburg.org.za/media_/Newsroom/Pages/2018%20News%20Articles/Mayor-Mashaba-administration-marks-2-years-in-multi-party-coalition-government.asp. Accessed 21 December 2020.

Kadima, D. 2014. An introduction to the politics of party alliances and coalitions in socially-divided Africa. *Journal of African Elections*, 13(1):1-24.

Kadima, D. & Lembani, S. 2006. "Making, unmaking and remaking political party coalitions in Malawi: Explaining the prevalence of office-seeking behaviour" in Kadima, D. *The politics of party coalitions in Africa*. Johannesburg: EISA, KAS.

Kapa, M.A. & Shale. 2014. Alliances, coalitions and the political system in Lesotho 2007-2012. *Journal of African Elections*, 13(1):93-114.

Kepe, T. & Ntsebeza, L. (eds). 2012. Rural Resistance in South Africa: The Mpondo Revolts after Fifty Years. Cape Town: University of Cape Town Press.

Kimberly, M. & Nkosi, N. 2019. Mongameli Bobani voted out as mayor of Nelson Mandela Bay. *Herald.* 05 December.

Kotze, J. 2016. How South Africa's Nelson Mandela Bay may be the ANC's mini-Waterloo. *The Conversation.* Available at: https://theconversation.com/how-south-africas-nelson-mandela-bay-may-be-the-ancs-mini-waterloo-58010. Accessed 19 September 2020.

Kumar, P. 2011. Zimbabwe: Good economic genes stunted by politics. *World Bank Blogs.* [Online]. Available at: https://worldbank.org/africacan/Zimbabwe-good-economic-genes-stunted-by-politics. Accessed 10 August 2020.

Kynoch, G. 2013. Reassessing transition violence: Voices from South Africa's township wars, 1990-4. *African Affairs*, 112(447):283-303.

Ledwaba, K. 2021. Free State mayor on her own as she faces motion of no confidence. *Sowetan.* 22 February.

Madisa, K. 2018. 'No data to support Mashaba's claim on hijacked buildings' - Africa Check. *Sowetan.* 31 July.

Mailovich, C. 2020. Tshwane 'is rudderless and has no service delivery', laments Makhura. *Business Day.* 6 March.

Makatile, D. 2016. High cost of Nkandla exceeds R246m. *Sunday Independent.* 7 February.

Maromo, J. 2016. No "Sputla", no vote, say ANC members. *Pretoria News.* 21 June.

Marx, K. 1843. *Critique of Hegel's Philosophy of Right* Cambridge University Press.

Maserumule, H.M. 2007. Conflicts between Directors-General and Ministers in South Africa 1994-2004: A 'postulative' approach. *Politikon*, 34(2):147-164.

Maserumule, H.M. 2011. Good governance in the new partnership for Africa's development (NEPAD): A Public Administration perspective. Doctor of Literature and Philosophy thesis. Pretoria: University of South Africa.

Maserumule, H.M. 2015. Why Biko's Black Consciousness philosophy resonates with youth today. *The Conversation.* Available at: https://theconversation.com/why-bikos-black-consciousness-philosophy-resonates-with-youth-today-46909.

Maserumule, H.M., Mokate, R. & Vil-Nkomo, S. 2016. *Tumultuous times for South Africa as it enters the era of coalition politics.* http://theconversation.com/tumultuous-times-for-south-africa-as-it-enters-the-era-of-coalition-politics-64312. Accessed 25 April 2020.

Masipa, T.S. 2017. The rise of multi-partyism in South Africa's political spectrum: the age of coalition and multi-party governance. Paper presented at the 2nd Annual International Conference on Public Administration and Development Alternatives 26-28 July 2017, Botswana.

Matlosa, K. & Shale, V. 2008. *Political Parties Programme Handbook.* Johannesburg: EISA.

McMillan, A. 2014. The causes of political party alliances and coalitions and their effects on national cohesion in India. *Journal of African Elections*, 13(1):118-206.

Mokgosi, K., Shai, K. & Ogunnubi, O. 2017. Local Government Coalition in Gauteng Province of South Africa: Challenges and opportunities. *Ubuntu*, 6(1): 37-57.

Mokhawa, G. 2011. Examining Zimbabwe's Global Political Agreement. *Southern African Peace and Security Studies*, 2(2):23-34.

Morifi, K. 2019. Does ANC have the moral authority to govern Tshwane? *Pretoria News.* 28 January.

Moshodi, J.M. 2018. Coalition politics: A new political landscape in South Africa. Masters Dissertation. University of Free State: Free State.

Müller, W. & Miller, B. 2005. "Coalition Government and Intra-Party Politics". ECPR Joint Sessions of Workshops, Workshop 25, Granada, 14-19 April 2005. Available at: https://ecpr.eu/Filestore/PaperProposal/c21c102fe9a1-4505-9339-d584eadbd73a.pdf. Accessed 2 May 2018.

Murambadoro, R. 2015. We cannot reconcile until the past has been acknowledged. *Accord.*

Mutisi, M. 2011. Beyond the signature: Appraisal of the Zimbabwe Global Political Agreement (GPA) and Implications for Intervention. *Accord*, 004.

National Democratic Institute. 2017. Coalitions: A Guide for Political Parties. Available at: https://www.ndi.org/sites/default/files/Flyer%2010.22_0.pdf

Ndletyana, M. 2018. Coalition councils: Origin, composition and impact on local government. *Journal of Public Administration*, 53(2):139 -141.

Nkosi, N. 2020. R1.6bn and counting - the cost of instability in Nelson Mandela Bay. *The Herald*. 13 October.

NUMSA. Available at: https://www.numsa.org.za/about/. Accessed 19 September 2020.

Olver, C. 2016. *State Capture at a local level: A Case Study of Nelson Mandela Bay*. Public Affairs Research Institute, 1-33.

Olver, C. 2017. *How to steal a city: The battle for Nelson Mandela Bay*. Johannesburg: Jonathan Ball Publishers.

Oyugi, O.W. 2006. Coalition politics and coalition governments in Africa. *Journal of Contemporary African Studies* 24(1).

Papaioannou, K.J. 2017. "Hunger makes a thief of any man": Poverty and crime in British colonial Asia. *European Review of Economic History*, 21(1): 1-28.

Paulse, J. 2018. Moody's upgrades NMB rating. *SABC News*. Available at: https://www.sabcnews.com/sabcnews/moodys-upgrades-nmb-rating/. Accessed 30 September 2020.

Ploch, L. 2010. Zimbabwe: Background. Congressional Research Service. Report for Congress. Available at: https://fas.org/sgp/crs/row/RL32723.pdf

Public Protector, 2020. *Report No. 13 of 2020/21 on an investigation into allegations of maladministration, improper or suspected improper conduct in the appointment of Mr. Previn Devalingam Govender to the position of Chief of Emergency by the Tshwane Metropolitan Municipality*. PDF. Public Protector South Africa. http://www.pprotect.org/?q=content/d-report-no-13-202021-investigation-allegations-maladministration-improper-or-suspected. News24. 2018. National Treasury steps in over 'interference' in procedures in Nelson Mandela Bay. *News24*. Available at: https://www.news24.com/news24/SouthAfrica/News/national-treasury-steps-in-over-interference-in-procedures-in-nelson-mandela-bay-20180905. Accessed 20 September 2020.

SAPA. 2013. Bring back death penalty: survey. *Times Live*. [Online]. Available at: https://www.timeslive.co.za/news/south-africa/2013-02-22-bring-back-death-penalty-survey/. Accessed 30 September 2020.

Sachikonye, L. 2011. *When a state turns on its citizens: 60 years of institutionalised violence in Zimbabwe*. Johannesburg: Jacana Media.

Sesant, S. 2016. ANC in Nelson Mandela Bay to resubmit councillor candidate lists. *Eyewitness News*. Available at: https://ewn.co.za/2016/06/16/ANC-in-Mandela-Bay-forced-to-resubmit-councillor-candidate-due-to-error. Accessed 30 August 2020.

Shaidi, E.W. 2013. Investigation into causes of service delivery protests in municipalities: A case study of Nelson Mandela Bay Municipality. Doctoral thesis. Department of Political and Governmental Studies. Nelson Mandela Metropolitan University.

Sithanen, R. 2003. Coalition politics under the tropics: Office seekers, power makers, nation building: A case study of Mauritius presented at EISA roundtable Strengthening Democracy through Coalition Building. Available at: https://aceproject.org/ero-en/topics/parties-andcandidates/mauritius.pdf

Smith-Hohn, J. 2009. *Unpacking the Zimbabwe Crisis: A Situation Report*. Institute for Security Studies.

Snider, L. 1987. Identifying the elements of state power: Where do we begin? *SAGE Journal*, 20(3).

Southall, R. 2013. *Liberation movements in power: Party and State in Southern Africa*. Suffolk: Boydell & Brewer.

Spies, D. 2017. Bobani: Urgent application struck from roll with costs. *News24*. https://www.news24.com/news24/SouthAfrica/News/bobani-urgent-application-dismissed-with-costs-20170919. Accessed 30 September 2020.

Statistics South Africa. 2016. Gross Domestic Product: First Quarter 2016. [Online] Available at: http://www.statssa.gov.za/publications/P0441/P04411stQuarter2016.pdf

Umraw, A. 2018. Makhura admits ANC has neglected coloured communities in Gauteng. *TimesLive*. Available at: https://www.timeslive.co.za/politics/

2018-07-20-makhura-admits-anc-has-neglected-coloured-communities-in-gauteng/. Accessed 28 February 2021.

Vorster, G. 2016. ANC could lose two very big metros in 2016: Expert. *BusinessTech*. Available at: https://businesstech.co.za/news/government/108533/anc-could-lose-two-very-big-metros-in-2016-expert/. Accessed 19 December 2020.

Wa Afrika, M. & Hofstatter, S. 2010. Bheki Cele's R500m police rental deal. *Sunday Times*. 1 August.

Wa Azania, M. 2014. *Memoirs of a Born Free: Reflections on the Rainbow Nation*. Johannesburg: Jacana Media.

Williamson, D.G. 1989. *The Third Reich*. New York: Bookwright Press.

World Bank. 2021. *The World Bank in Rwanda*. [Online] Available at: https://worldbank.org/en/country/rwanda/overview. Accessed 8 August 2020.

Xaba, V. 2013. Zamdela rejects merger. *Sowetan*. 21 January.

ZADHR. 2008. Cases of post-election violence continue to escalate. Available at: http://www.kubatana.net/html/archive/hr/080415zadhr.asp?sector=ELEC. Accessed 01 June 2020.

Zimbabwe Lawyers for Human Rights. 2008. Violent retributive action against innocent Zimbabweans by state agents on the increase. Available at: http://www.kubatana.net/html/archive/hr/080417zlhr.asp?sector=ELEC. Accessed 01 June 2020.

INDEX

A

ANC Youth League 38, 58, 89, 91
AZAPO 99, 107, 108

B

Bundestag 97

C

City of Cape Town 52, 54
City of Ekurhuleni 12, 14, 15, 38, 39, 41, 64, 65, 66,
67, 68, 70, 71, 72, 73, 74, 75, 76, 77, 78, 80, 81, 87,
92, 93, 98, 100, 108, 109
City of eThekwini 67
City of Johannesburg 10, 14, 15, 38, 39, 41, 42, 43,
44, 45, 46, 57, 68, 73, 81, 92, 98
City of Tshwane 10, 13, 14, 15, 38, 39, 41, 45, 46, 47,
48, 49, 50, 51, 57, 58, 62, 68, 73, 84, 88, 96, 98, 109
COGTA 48

D

Dominant-party system 4, 5, 6

E

Economic Freedom Fighters 34, 85

F

Freedom Charter 106
Freedom Front Plus 59, 60, 61, 62, 63, 64, 72, 99

G

Gauteng Province 13, 36, 46, 52, 64, 66, 69, 73, 75,
76, 79, 88
Germany 7, 10, 11, 97, 98
Global Political Agreement 15, 17, 19, 21, 26
Government of National Unity 2, 15, 16, 17, 21, 22,
23, 27, 96
Gukurahundi 18, 19, 26

H

Hegelian 3

I

Independent Electoral Commission 12, 33, 36, 42, 59,
64, 106
India 6, 11, 87, 109
Inkatha Freedom Party 106

J

Japan 6, 87
Johannesburg 10, 13, 14, 15, 22, 38, 39, 41, 42, 43,
44, 45, 46, 57, 62, 68, 73, 81, 92, 98

K

Kenya 11

L

Lesotho 4, 12

INDEX

M

Mauritius 7, 9, 10, 26
Metsimaholo Local Municipality 37, 41, 58, 59, 62, 63, 90, 109
Movement for Democratic Change 17
Mpumalanga Province 29, 63

N

National assembly 1, 2, 6, 27, 35, 56, 95, 108
Nelson Mandela Bay Metropolitan Municipality 14, 15, 37, 52
Nkandla 35, 36, 70, 75

O

One-party system 4, 5, 12

P

Philosophy of Right 3
Plurality 14, 37, 64, 88, 89, 102

R

Ready to Govern 94

S

South African Communist Party 61, 90
Southern Africa Development Community 16

T

Two-party system 4, 5

U

Unemployment 17, 29, 30, 31, 32, 33, 34, 72
Union of the Soviet Socialist Republics 18, 106

V

Violence 2, 11, 17, 18, 19, 20, 21, 22, 23, 24, 25, 26, 31, 34, 51, 64, 65, 84, 103
Voting 20, 23, 33, 40, 45, 56, 63, 69, 71, 74, 75, 105

W

Western Cape Province 37
Workers and Socialist Party 105

X

Xenophobia 43

Z

ZANU-PF 17, 18, 19, 20, 21, 22, 23, 24, 25, 26, 27, 96, 97, 102
ZINASU 24

www.ingramcontent.com/pod-product-compliance
Lightning Source LLC
Chambersburg PA
CBHW080555270326
41929CB00019B/3319